HIS OWN RECEIVED HIM NOT

HIS OWN RECEIVED HIM NOT

Donald Grey Barnhouse

Alliance Publishing

600 Eden Road
Lancaster, PA 17601

Contents

Preface

Everything that can be known about the Lord Jesus Christ is to be found in the Bible. There is no other source of materials. One of the proofs that the Bible is the inspired Word of God is that there is no possibility of exhausting it. Each succeeding generation finds the Word as fresh and new as though it were just written.

Any study which brings more light from the Book itself, comparing Scripture with Scripture, enhancing and revealing our Lord the more, is sufficiently justified.

When the life and work of Christ are seen through the first word of John 1:12, "But… ", and when His teaching is seen through the parables spoken on that great Saturday afternoon when He sat in a boat on the lake, the whole Bible, from Genesis to Revelation, begins to be a clear and limpid stream of truth. Then even a novice may hope to understand it in its great outlines, and the deepest student will realize that it can never be fully comprehended until we know as we are known.

D. G. B

1
HE CAME TO HIS OWN: THE JEWS

We are more and more amazed that no student of the Bible, so far as we know, has ever approached the life of the Lord Jesus Christ from the point of view of a verse recorded in the first chapter of the Gospel according to John, which is given to us as an explanation of that life. There we read, "He came unto his own, and his own received him not. But as many as received him, to them gave he power [right, authority], to become the sons of God, even to them that believe on his name: which were born, not of blood, nor of the will of the flesh, nor of the will of man, but of God" (John 1:11-13).

The years of ministry of the Lord Jesus are divided into two distinct parts, during which He was doing two absolutely different things. In the first part, He was approaching His own, the Jews. This period came to an abrupt conclusion. After a definite break, when His own received Him not, He began offering the Gospel of grace to the whole world.

Hundreds of thousands of books and pamphlets and sermons have been written about the Lord Jesus Christ. The authors of many of them are men who refuse to believe in Him. They profess to find errors in His teaching and write in order to seek to disprove Him. He overshadows the thinking of men, and they are forced to consider Him, whether they will or not.

We know, of course, that most difficulties that many people have with the Bible come from the fact that they are not born again; but sometimes even Christians are led into false thinking through their failure to understand certain elemental truths concerning the life of the Lord Jesus Christ. Many difficulties in the minds of those who study the life and person of our Lord, and many supposed contradictions in the Bible, will be removed by a careful study of His turning from His own, the Jews, to as many as received Him.

Men have fallen into great error when preparing biographical studies of Jesus Christ, especially as they seek to consider His life as they would that of any ordinary man. When a man wishes to write the biography of one of the great men of the earth, he collects his materials and writes his study in some orderly manner, generally in the sequence of strict chronology. God did not give us this sort of biography in the Gospels, but something entirely different.

God has given us four portraits of the Lord Jesus Christ in the four Gospels in order to present entirely different aspects of His work. He has arranged His materials in the order in which we find them so that we might get these great views of the Lord without thinking this is a merely human life that is being reported.

There is a difference between a biography and a monograph. The biography is an attempt at the appraisal of a life from birth to death. A monograph, when written of a life, presents merely one phase of that life. Books have been written concerning certain great men which omit entire phases of their lives, simply because the writers were limiting themselves to one particular aspect of their theme. One volume may portray a leader as a statesman; another may present him as a military strategist; still another may write of his home life or the steps in his rise to political power. To accuse these writers of bad faith because one of them omits certain events or refers to these only in support of one thesis, while another uses them to illustrate quite different points, is to ignore the flexibility of life. Moreover, this procedure ignores the fact that a single incident may have ramifications that bind it to many phases of living.

In the same way, we may approach the four Gospels and see what was the divine purpose in having these different Gospels. The moment that we demonstrate a valid purpose in back of the different accounts, we lift from them any thought of discrepancy. They are not four biographies, drawing their materials from various sources or recording events which the writers have imperfectly remembered. They were written by holy men who spoke and wrote as they were carried along by the Holy Spirit (cf. 2 Pet. 1:21). After all, the Holy Spirit is the One who, out of the full life of the Lord Jesus, is drawing the Gospel authors' attention to the events that will show Him in some of the different aspects of His work.

For these reasons, any attempted harmony of the Gospels is perhaps one of the most futile things in all theology. We have read many such books. There is no necessity for or human possibility of a chronological harmony of the four Gospels. God never meant that everything in the four Gospels should dovetail into everything else. To be sure, frequently a detail in one account will substantiate a fact in another. However, if harmonization had been the overall intent, we should expect one Gospel and not four.

If the study of the life of Christ is begun with the thought that He could never have preached the same sermon more than once under different circumstances, then the Bible can certainly be made to contradict itself. Consider the majestic prayer which begins, "Our Father who art in heaven, Hallowed be thy name … " (Matt. 6:9 RSV). Matthew records our Lord saying this in the midst of the Sermon on the Mount to a multitude of people who were gathered around the

Lord. Luke records it, with slightly different wording, but in an entirely different setting, spoken long after the Sermon on the Mount to a small group of His disciples (see Luke 11:2-4). If any attempt be made to reconcile the accounts of Matthew and Luke on the theory that they are different stories of the same incident, there is hopeless contradiction.

But if we get away from any idea of harmonizing events of the Gospels, realizing that our Lord often retold His parables and outlined His great teachings on different occasions, all difficulty vanishes. Indeed, some of the miracles were duplicated in almost identical circumstances. Our Lord fed five thousand people on one occasion and four thousand on another, each with a small number of loaves and fishes. Other incidents are also repeated, as when the feet of Jesus were anointed by Mary of Bethany as recorded in three of the Gospels and when on an earlier occasion they were anointed in the house of the Pharisee by a woman who was a sinner.

Now, some people think that these accounts contradict each other. Take, for instance, the record given concerning Mary of Bethany. When we realize that anointing of the feet was as common an occurrence in those days as asking a guest to take off his hat and coat is in our day, to say that such a narrative contradicts another account becomes more absurd than ever.

But it is not our purpose to pick out the detailed charges which have been made upon Scripture in order to point out how unwarranted are these attacks. We wish to show that there is a method of understanding the life of Christ which simplifies the whole discussion and removes many of the problems with a single stroke.

The two parts of Christ's ministry mentioned at the beginning should not be compared. "But ..." is a dividing point that is not to be treated lightly. Naturally, there will be some statements which Christ made as He came to the Jews as Messiah which will differ from those which were made after He turned from His own to as many as received Him. Yet all of these statements are true. Such statements should not be compared with each other.

For instance, someone might write a story of a young doctor. In the first part of the story you might find a description of the doctor's work, saying that he worked at night and slept in the daytime. Later you might find it written that he worked during the day and slept by night. These statements are contradictory only if they apply to the same period of his life. But if the one speaks of the years during which he was an intern, and the other of the time when he was master of his own practice, there is no contradiction, since they apply to different periods.

Therefore, to understand the life of the Lord Jesus Christ, we must realize that He came, first of all to the Jews, and that He came only as the Jewish Messiah could come to that people. Then something occurred which changes the whole picture. Now He offers the Gospel "to as many as received him ... even to them that believe on his name." There is a world of difference. Almost all the puzzling elements in the teachings of the Lord Jesus Christ resolve themselves immediately if this is understood.

How can the seeming "pacifistic" statements of the Sermon on the Mount be reconciled with the declaration, "I came not to send peace, but a sword." (Matt. 10:34)? And how shall we explain the change in method that He enjoined upon His disciples? He sent them forth in great haste, telling them that they were not to take time to provide extra clothes, money, food or other necessities. Later on He reversed this command. He said unto them, "When I sent you without purse, and scrip, and shoes, lacked ye any thing? And they said, Nothing. Then said he unto them, But now, he that hath a purse, let him take it, and likewise his scrip: and he that hath no sword, let him sell his garment and buy one..." (Luke 22:35-36). All of this can be understood only if we realize that He came, first of all, to the Jews, and that subsequently He stopped presenting Himself as the Messiah of Israel and took His way to the cross to become the Savior of the world.

In writing of the privileges of Israel, the Holy Spirit says, "To whom pertaineth the adoption, and the glory, and the covenants, and the giving of the law, and the service of God, and the promises; Whose are the fathers, and of whom as concerning the flesh Christ came, who is over all…" (Rom. 9:4-5). This gives us the definition of "His own."

The first aspect of His coming was unto His own. This can have but one meaning when it is considered in the light of the entire Bible. He came to His people, the Jews, offering to do the work of the Messiah. The reason that His people rejected Him is clear. They had a preconceived idea of what the Messiah should be and do. Their foregone conclusion was built upon a superficial reading of the Scriptures. They were ready to accept a Messiah who would fulfill their idea of what he should be, but they were not ready to accept a Messiah Who came with the truths that Christ preached.

Their whole attitude grew from their interpretation of the prophecies of the Old Testament concerning the return of the Lord Jesus Christ. There can be no doubt, and Jew and Christian believe alike in this, that the Old Testament contains many statements, which, if interpreted literally, can mean but one thing. God has promised that He would send a Messiah, Who would end the scattering of Israel and bring them back to their land in triumph. There is to be a literal Kingdom over which the Messiah shall rule from Jerusalem, reestablishing the throne of David and ruling in power and glory. "In those days it shall come to pass, that ten men shall take hold out of all languages of the nations, even shall take hold of the skirt of him that is a Jew, saying, We will go with you: for we have heard that God is with you" (Zech. 8:23). Or, as Isaiah says:

And many people shall go and say, Come ye, and let us go up to the mountain of the LORD, to the house of the God of Jacob; and he will teach us of his ways, and we will walk in his paths: for out of Zion shall go forth the law, and the word of the LORD from Jerusalem. And he shall judge among the nations, and shall rebuke many people: and they shall beat their swords into plowshares, and their spears into pruning hooks: nation shall not lift up sword against nation, neither shall they learn war any more (Isa. 2:3-4).

The Jews were looking for this and this alone.

When Jesus came, He made a bona fide offer of this Kingdom and power to the people of Israel. But they were not willing to accept it on His terms. He knew before He came that they would refuse it—knew it from all eternity; hence, there are prophecies which speak of His coming to die for us. Both were fully known to Him in His eternal plan; but the fact of His foreknowledge in no case alters the fact that He came and offered the literal Kingdom to Israel.

Let us consider, first of all, the words of John the Baptist who preceded Jesus as the forerunner of the Messiah. If it be thought for a moment that Jesus came only to die, without making the honest offer of the Kingdom to Israel, how will you explain the ministry of John the forerunner? To us, the preaching of John is one of the greatest proofs that the Lord was presenting the earthly Kingdom to the Jews. This is sufficient proof even if we did not have the definite words of the text: "He came unto his own, and his own received him not..."

There are, as anyone can easily find with the simplest study, two lines of prophecy in the Old Testament concerning the coming of Christ. In one set of passages, He is to come as a splendid, resistless sovereign, ruling with a rod of iron and dashing His enemies to pieces as a potter's vessel (cf. Ps. 2). In the other line of prophecy He is to come, meek and lowly, riding upon an ass, led as a lamb to the slaughter, and dumb before those who persecuted Him (cf. Isa. 53). He comes to be wounded for our transgressions and bruised for our iniquities, to be cut off for the sins of His people. Forsaken of the Father, He is to fulfill all the types of the offering of the sacrifices upon the altar.

When John the Baptist came to announce the Messiah, upon which set of prophecies did he draw for his preaching? A careful analysis of all the passages of John's ministry up to the time he baptized Jesus Christ reveals the following facts: His quotations from the Old Testament are all prophecies of what we call the second coming of Christ, even though he came before the first coming of Christ. John spoke of Christ as Savior only in one passage, and that on the day of the baptism of the Lord; and most significantly it is only in the fourth Gospel that this is recorded. It can also be demonstrated that John the Baptist did not understand what he was saying when he cried, "Behold the Lamb of God, which taketh away the sin of the world" (John 1:29); for later, when he was in prison, he sent disciples to ask the Lord if He, Jesus, were really the One that should come, or if another was to be expected (see Matt. 11:2-3).

But in his earlier ministry, John spoke of the Messiah as the Judge and King Who should come. "Prepare ye the way of Jehovah; make His paths straight." This is why John spoke to the Pharisees, calling them a generation of vipers, and saying, "Who hath warned you to flee from the wrath to come?" The symbols that John used were symbols of judgment. "And now also the axe is laid unto the root of the trees: therefore every tree which bringeth not forth good fruit is hewn down, and cast into the fire" (Matt. 3:10). This is parallel to the later prophecy of Christ that the tares would be gathered out of the field of wheat, and would be burned. It is clearly the definite teaching of the work of our Lord as judge of the earth, when He comes again.

Another symbol used by John in speaking of the ministry of the Lord, Whom he had come to announce, was that His "fan is in his hand, and he will thoroughly purge his floor…" (Matt. 3:12). This image seems strange to us, under modern conditions of agriculture, but it is easily understandable when we know the methods of preparing wheat that were used in the days of Christ; indeed, these methods are still in use in certain parts of the world today.

I recall traveling far out on the high plateau of Asia Minor when we came to a place where a farmer was threshing his wheat. When the grain had been trodden, a man took a pitchfork and tossed the grain in the air. A light wind carried the chaff away and the grain fell into a pile at his feet. Little by little the threshing floor was cleansed of its chaff. If the wind had grown too strong or too calm, the man would not have been able to separate the wheat from the chaff. He would have been forced to await a favorable wind.

Now do you see the point of the prophecy of John the Baptist? He said that the Christ, Who was to follow him, would carry His fan with Him, and so He would be able to purge the floor thoroughly of all its chaff. The Lord is Master of His own winds of judgment. He is not dependent upon the moods of man or the forces of nature. His fan will do its work. The chaff will be blown out from among the wheat. The passage concludes by saying that He will "gather his wheat into the garner; but he will burn up the chaff with unquenchable fire" (Matt. 3:12).

Now the remarkable point about all these prophecies made or quoted by John the Baptist, is that they refer to that work of Christ which is yet future. How are we to account for this? There are only two possible explanations, and only one of these is compatible with the dignity of the plan of God. The one explanation is that John the Baptist was abandoned by God to his own fallible reason, and that John made his own choice of the passages in the Old Testament which refer to the Messiah, and thus was mistaken in what he said and did. To accept such a theory would be to admit that there might be many other portions of the Bible absolutely untrustworthy. And we must not forget that it is said of John: "…he will be filled with the Holy Spirit, even from his mother's womb" (Luke 1:15 RSV). This bars any interpretation which would detract from the authority of John's message.

The other and true explanation is simply this. The Lord Jesus Christ came at the outset of His ministry offering the Kingdom to the Jews. He said that He was the Messiah. Again and again, they came to Him asking Him to tell them who He was. When He did tell them, they were not convinced. He said that He was God, and for this cause they took up stones to stone Him, because that He, being a man, (as they thought), made Himself equal with God (cf. John 5:18).

Finally, He refused to reiterate what He had said so often. We read in the fourth Gospel that when they asked Him once more who He was, He replied, "Even the same that I said unto you from the beginning" (John 8:25). He came offering to establish the Kingdom in power and glory provided they were willing to accept His principles of righteousness. It was as the forerunner of this phase of the work of Christ that John the Baptist came. It would not have fitted into the harmony of the plan if John had spoken merely of the redemptive work of Christ. The point of the honest presentation of the Kingdom to Israel would have been obscured. But when the leaders of Israel came to John and asked him if he were the Messiah, "And he confessed, and denied not; but confessed, I am not the Christ" (John 1:20). All he would claim to be was a voice, crying in the wilderness.

There is a great difference between the voice and the Word. Christ was the eternal Word, come to perform the work of redemption. But since God's plan includes not merely the offer of the Gospel to all the race but also the specific fulfilling in detail of all His promises to the Jews, it was necessary that the forerunner announce the Lord as the Messiah of Israel, and that Christ should come, first of all, unto His own.

There is a great contrast between the early message of Jesus which was the same as John's message of repentance and His later message which prepares the way for the great doctrinal utterances to be found in the epistles of Paul. There is a great difference between the Gospel of the Kingdom and the Gospel of grace. The Gospel of the Kingdom is a threat because of approaching judgment. Men are warned to repent because the Kingdom of Heaven is at hand. John's ethical message was based on the nearness of the wrath to come. Men were warned to bring forth fruits meet for repentance. Those who had abundance of goods were to divide with those who had none. Petty officials were warned against betraying the public trust. Soldiers were told that they were not to pillage, but to be content with their wages. This was not unlike the early ministry of the Lord Jesus. It was primarily an ethical message. "Now after that John was put in prison, Jesus came into Galilee, preaching the gospel of the kingdom of God, And saying, The time is fulfilled, and the kingdom of God is at hand: repent ye, and believe the gospel" (Mark 1:14-15).

This was far different from the message of Christ's later ministry when He announced that He was come to seek and to save that which was lost (see Luke 19:10), and that He came not to be ministered unto but to minister and to give His life a ransom for many (see Matt. 20:28). This is the early announcement of that which we shall find stated so strongly by the Spirit of God through the Apostle,

> Being justified freely by his grace through the redemption that is in
> Christ Jesus: Whom God hath set forth to be a propitiation [literally,
> a mercy–seat, that is, a blood sacrifice] through faith in his blood,

to declare his righteousness for the remission of sins that are past, through the forbearance of God; to declare, I say, at this time his righteousness: that he might be just and the justifier of him which believeth in Jesus (Rom. 3:24–26).

The essence of Christ's teaching in the first part of His ministry, that in which He was offering the Kingdom to the Jews, His own people, is to be found in the Sermon on the Mount.

2
THE CONSTITUTION OF THE KINGDOM

We can never understand the Lord Jesus Christ unless we realize fully that He was a Jew, and that He came unto His own as the Jewish Messiah. Why, then, did His own not receive Him? It was the preaching of the Sermon on the Mount that caused the Jewish leaders to reject His claims.

Certain schools of theology have attempted to deny salvation by the death of Jesus Christ on the grounds that Paul's religious ideas are not to be accepted in preference to the teachings of Jesus Christ. A few years ago a nationally known preacher said that there were two kinds of Christianity. The one was the religion *of* Jesus and His way of living, while the other was the religion *about* Jesus which was doctrinal. He implied that the religion *of* Jesus was to be preferred to that *about* Jesus. If this man had understood the difference between the first and the last parts of the ministry of Christ, he could never have made such an error. For, undoubtedly, by the religion *of* Jesus he meant that which was preached in the first part of His ministry, as summarized in the Sermon on the Mount; and by the religion *about* Jesus, he meant that which was prepared by Christ's great statements concerning Himself after He had turned away from the first part of His course in order to do an entirely new thing.

The background of this rejection of Jesus by the Jews is to be found in the situation which prevailed in the land at the moment when the Lord began His work. Some sixty years before the birth of Christ, Rome, under Pompey, conquered Syria, and in the following year entered Jerusalem. From that time the Jews were a people under bondage. Roman governors ruled the land; Roman procurators watched every portion of the country; Roman taxes were collected from the people with the help of renegade Jews, the publicans; Roman legions were quartered in the cities; Roman coins with the image of Caesar were in every Jewish hand. This situation was intolerable to the brave hearts of a people who had been trained through centuries of liberty; and the fact that their immediate ancestors had known captivity in no way reduced the longings that had been built up through a millennium of growth in power. In fact, the trials of the nation had but whetted their desire for a deliverer who should come to free them from the yoke of the enemy.

The greatest factor of all was that the center of their religion was their hope of a Messiah. This hope was the heart that pumped the lifeblood through the nation and made them look with expectation at every figure that rose in the slightest degree above the ordinary mass of men. This is demonstrated in the historical fact that there were many false Messiahs. The leaders made it easy for these pretenders to gain a following. Anyone can see that the questions which were asked of both Jesus and John the Baptist were stock questions on the lips of the religious leaders who sent their delegations to search out these amazing figures for the usual interview. "Art thou the Christ?" "Art thou Elijah?" "Art thou that prophet?" These were the questions which were put to John and to Jesus, and probably to many others. The counterfeits, of course, were waiting for such an opportunity to announce their pretentious claims, counting the plaudits of the mob as sufficient prize for a day and a night, even if the morning brought death. Do we not have in our own day those who are almost willing to commit murder, providing their pictures can be in the tabloids while they occupy the central scene in the court room, even though it be but one step to the death chamber? Whatever the consequences, their weak minds have had their moment of dominance.

When John the Baptist came, these same questions were put to him. "And he confessed, and denied not; but confessed, I am not the Christ" (John 1:20). All he would claim for himself was the role which God had marked out for him, "I am the voice of one crying in the wilderness, Make straight the way of the Lord, as said the prophet Esaias" (John 1:23).

When the Lord Jesus began His ministry the same questions were asked. The story of His earliest contacts with those who were to be His disciples reveals that they were convinced of His Messiahship from the beginning. Andrew, in running to find his brother Simon Peter, who was to play so great a part in the movement that was to follow, came with the breathless words, "We have found the Messiah" (John 1:41). This was spoken even before the first of the miracles took place. When the water had been turned into wine and the nobleman's son healed, the whole populace came in multitudes for the sake of the healing, and later, for the sake of bread. In a thousand homes He was discussed. A multitude whispered that He was Elijah returned, or even the Messiah.

When the Lord Jesus proclaimed that He was the Messiah, there were in the minds of some of His hearers certain prejudices that had to be overcome. When counterfeits are in circulation, many people look askance at good money. There had been false Messiahs, and the people who had followed them had perished under the heel of Rome. The legions were there for the purpose of keeping peace, and insurrections were soon put down.

The mob was fully prepared, psychologically, for the advent of a deliverer. But they were prepared only for a Messiah who would fit certain preconceived notions which they had formed. Every supposed Messiah had to be measured by their hard and fast pattern. They were guided by two considerations: there was the psychology of despair which demanded a strong leader capable of breaking the Roman yoke, and there was the psychology of sin which demanded a Messiah who would keep the ruling classes in power without asking of them any change in heart.

A modern analogy can be drawn from the events of 1917 in Russia. Leon Trotsky has painted a wonderful picture of the summer days in Russia between the time of the early revolution and the final triumph of the Bolsheviks. The possessing classes were looking for a leader. But that leader had to have two qualifications. He had to have sufficient military power to dominate the force of the German enemy from without and the worker enemy from within. Also, he had to be inclined to confirm the landlords and the generals in their vested interests. They gave their fealty to Kerensky and to Kornilov. They wanted to remain in the midst of their debauchery and let these men do it all without any help from them. When Kornilov's rebellion was started in late August it came to a miserable end because his supposed allies in Petersburg were either drunk or occupied with some orgy. Kerensky was too often under the influence of dope, and the whole pyramid, which had stood on its point too long, toppled over.

While the scribes and the Pharisees were not stupefied in vice they were, nevertheless, drunk with a wine that is more heady than the vintages of the fields. It is hard to imagine any group more filled with pride and arrogance than these leaders of Israel in the days when Jesus of Nazareth came preaching the Gospel of the Kingdom.

The multitudes followed Jesus Christ; and as He sat on the brow of a hill with the crowd about Him, eagerly awaiting His message, "And he opened his mouth, and taught them, saying, Blessed are the poor in spirit: for theirs is the kingdom of heaven" (Matt. 5:2-3). These words must have cut like a whip across the minds of the unregenerate listeners.

If there is anything that a man cannot know by himself, it is that he must take a place of humility before God. There is a natural repulsion against the idea of being poor in spirit. Man is rich in pride and he wants to shield himself from any thought of poverty of resources, whether of strength, of morals, or of intellect. This is the direct statement of the Lord Jesus that there must be a miraculous change in the lives of men if they are to participate with Him in His Kingdom glory. How can a man see himself properly in the sight of God? It is only when we have understood the great truths of the holiness of God and the sinfulness of sin that we are forced to flee from ourselves, pleading that we have sinned and come short of the glory of God. We then ask God to effect within us the miracle of grace which He now promises to perform on the basis of the death of Jesus Christ, the Substitute who died in our place.

But when these words came from the lips of our Lord Jesus Christ they were heard by the proud and the arrogant. Were they not the chosen people? Did they not have the full assurance that they were the special objects of God's love? Little by little, they had come to presume upon their position under law which was, at the same time, a position under grace, since they had the access to the altar through their priests, and the way of salvation through the sacrifice. But they were like that Pharisee who thought, because he fasted and tithed and was not like a wretched publican, that he was not under the wrath of God. He was continuing in sin, presuming upon the outward form of a misunderstood covenant.

"Blessed are the meek: for they shall inherit the earth" (Matt. 5:5). Again the whip lashed. The meek shall inherit the earth? What nonsense! These Pharisees knew that they had taken possession of the earth, but they also knew that they had not received it through meekness. The only humility which they knew was that which served as a cloak for their grasping thievery.

Now, the Lord is announcing the righteous principle. Later, He will strip the mask from these alleged holy men and leave them no basis for their hollow pretence. He will say to them, "Woe unto you, scribes and Pharisees, hypocrites! for ye devour widows' houses, and for a pretence make long prayer: therefore ye shall receive the greater damnation" (Matt. 23:14). But in the Sermon on the Mount, the Kingdom offer is being made. He is announcing that in the Kingdom when He shall reign upon the earth, possession will be vested in those who are meek.

We are not to think of this word in any unfavorable sense. Meekness is not fawning servility. It is that quality in a man which proves him to be patient under injuries, not vain or haughty or resentful; forbearing, kind. In truth, it is the gift of God and is a part of the new life that is given to us at the new birth when we have accepted the Lord Jesus Christ as our own personal Savior. All that an unsaved man may ever know of meekness is the humility, like that of Dickens' interesting character, Uriah Heep, whose sniveling mockery lasted as long as there was a shred to his mask. Any meekness that the world can know will differ from this only in degree, but it will always be of this kind, for true meekness is the fruit of the indwelling life of the Lord Jesus Christ (see Gal. 5:22).

It would be possible to go through that great discourse, the Sermon on the Mount, phrase by phrase, and show how every part must have cut to the very quick the leaders of Israel. But we need only to move on to the climax. We need not consider the impression on their evil hearts when the spotless Christ looked upon them and said, "Blessed are the pure in heart: for they shall see God" (Matt. 5:8). They knew their hearts well enough to wince at the words. They should have been the salt of the earth and the light of the world. Their own consciences were able to tell them that, in their case, the salt had lost its savor, and that their sputtering wicks gave forth no light. They were indeed "blind leaders of the blind."

But the climax was reached when He named them, and in naming them destroyed the standards which they had so carefully erected. They had taken the law and whittled it down throughout the centuries. In place of the simple commandments that cannot be misunderstood, they had substituted a complex commentary that enabled them to disobey the law as God gave it and yet salve their own consciences.

The Lord Jesus often spoke of this. He used as an illustration, in one case, the fact that they made the Word of God of none effect by saying that a gift was *Corban*. In practical terms this was as follows. The law said, "Honour thy father and thy mother ..." Certainly the simplest understanding of this definite commandment would include caring for them and providing for them when they were old. But there were hard-hearted children who did not want to do this. So they got around it by saying that their resources were *Corban*, that is, dedicated to the temple. Therefore they could not give them to their parents to supply their needs. Thus they evaded the commandment and, of course, that which was dedicated to the temple, more often than not, was not paid. So they kept their resources as though they were holding them in trust for God, but they themselves collected the interest!

It was to minds capable of this type of hypocrisy that the Lord Jesus said, "Think not that I am come to destroy the law, or the prophets: I am not come to destroy, but to fulfill. For verily I say unto you, Till heaven and earth pass, one jot or one tittle shall in no wise pass from the law, till all be fulfilled" (Matt. 5:17-18). The context proves the real meaning that Christ gave to this statement. He was announcing that God would not diminish by one iota all the righteous demands of the law. These men were sinners. They knew that they were sinners, and recognizing that they had never kept the law, they tried to find their way around the law.

Christ came to say that God would in no wise lower His mandate, but that He would find a way to raise man above the demands of the law. The Old Testament had presented the moral perfections of God's demands, but men had failed to understand. The Jews, "being ignorant of God's righteousness, and going about to establish their own righteousness, have not submitted themselves unto the righteousness of God" (Rom. 10:3). They had grown familiar with the form of words contained in the law and, little by little, had built a detour around it, until they had made it possible to sin with impunity and keep the conscience quiet.

The Sermon on the Mount brought all this to an end. Christ effectively blocked every detour and brought men back to the standards of God's holiness. Had they come to think that God could be satisfied with the keeping of the mere letter of the law? He would take the whole question of man's relationship with God out of the realm of acts and into the realm of thought. They had thought that it was necessary to have a *corpus delicti* in order to be a murderer, but He demonstrated that man killed because he was a murderer at heart, and that guilt came with the thinking. They had thought that it was necessary to go to the final act of contamination in order to be guilty of adultery, but He demonstrated that defilement lay in the heart. It followed then, that those who had never had a physical victim for their thoughts were just as guilty in the sight of God as those who had carried their thoughts to the full perpetration of the deed.

All this appears in His message which must have brought the wrath of the leaders to a veritable frenzy. Later we read that they "held a council against him, how they might destroy him" (Matt. 12:14). He had given them cause enough, from their point of view. For unless they were willing to adopt God's point of view, the only thing to do was to get rid of Christ as soon as possible. That is true for men today, also. If you do not want to adopt God's point of view, get Christ and all He stands for out of your thinking. Go your own way. Dash yourself against His law. You cannot break the commandments, but you can break yourself against the commandments.

Now He uttered the words that brought these men under God's light and also under the gaze of the people:

> Whosoever therefore shall break one of these least commandments, and shall teach men so, he shall be called the least in the kingdom of heaven: but whosoever shall do and teach them, the same shall be called great in the kingdom of heaven. For I say unto you, That except your righteousness shall exceed the righteousness of the scribes and Pharisees, ye shall in no case enter into the kingdom of heaven (Matt. 5:19-20).

We must not be deceived by the meaning which has been added to the word "Pharisee" through the years since Christ spoke these words. That name was a badge of honor until Christ spoiled it. Linen may appear white until you place it on the new fallen snow. When Christ, the light and whiteness of God, had stood beside the Pharisees for three years, the name thenceforth took on a terrible meaning and the word now stings if it be applied to any man—Pharisee! What an indictment!

Yet Paul in his day, appealing to accepted human standards, still used his title of Pharisee as a defense of honor. When he made his famous plea before Agrippa he could find no better argument than to say, "My manner of life from my youth ... know all the Jews ... that after the most straitest sect of our religion I lived a Pharisee" (Acts 26:4-5). And when he wished to tell the Philippian church that his life could be compared with any to his own profit he said, "If any other man thinketh that he hath whereof he might trust in the flesh, I more: Circumcised the eighth day, of the stock of Israel, of the tribe of Benjamin, an Hebrew of the Hebrews; as touching the law, a Pharisee" (Phil. 3:4-5).

These men were the finest in the community beyond any shadow of a doubt. They had dominated society and established their standards of morality. They held to these standards so firmly that they were beyond human reproach. It took the Son of God to pierce the barriers within which they had entrenched themselves. They gained distinction and praise by their observance of the external rights of their religion, and were very proud of their good works. They were marked by their great orthodoxy, which was a slavish faithfulness to their code rather than to God's. Instead of majestic tones of thunder which smote all hearts from Sinai when God spoke, "Thou shalt have no other gods before me," theirs was the puny tinkle of ordinances concerning the washing of pots and pans. If we could draw any kind of analogy in our civilization it would have to be with the leaders in all professions. The Pharisees would have included in their ranks the leading members of the bench and bar. The most honored among the bankers, the greatest professors, the most renowned philosophers, the best among the moralists and ethical leaders—all these would have been counted among the Pharisees.

So when the Lord Jesus turned to the crowd and said, "Except your righteousness shall exceed the righteousness of the scribes and the Pharisees," He was saying, "Except you shall have a code and an accomplishment better than anything the best of earth have produced, you shall in no wise enter the Kingdom of Heaven." This is Christ's verdict about the possibility of salvation through human accomplishment. It was for this reason that they were not ready to receive Him as Messiah. They wanted a Messiah; they were waiting eagerly for a Messiah. This is shown by a verse concerning John the Baptist. With his preaching the thoughts of men were excited and we read, "And as the people were in expectation, and all men mused in their hearts of John, whether he were the Christ or not" (Luke 3:15).

But they wanted a Messiah who would accept their standards, or at least not disturb them. When He comes again, the Lord Jesus will establish a Kingdom that is based on righteousness. The Sermon on the Mount is the constitution of that Kingdom. Then the poor in spirit, who are willing to accept God's estimate of character and conduct, will indeed inherit the Kingdom of Heaven. The mourners, those who are sad because of the terrible conditions of the earth today, shall be comforted. The merciful shall obtain mercy. The pure in heart shall see God. "The earth shall be full of the knowledge of the LORD, as the waters cover the sea" (Isa. 11:9).

There is one outstanding similarity between the attitude of the Pharisees and that of men and women in our day. They thought that if they lived up to their own artificial standards of righteousness, they would be acceptable before God. Our righteousness must exceed any righteousness that can be measured by man. The best that man can do can take him to Hell but it can never take him to Heaven. Heaven is too holy to be entered on any such basis of man's works.

It is idle to speculate on what would have happened had the Pharisees and other leaders accepted Jesus as the Messiah and bowed before His standards. Whether He could have found some way to impute righteousness to their account, or not, is a question not worthy of our discussion. We are bound to the relentless turning of the actual history of men and events. The fact is that they rejected the Lord Jesus Christ. His doctrine was poison to their unregenerate hearts. They held council how they might destroy Him. Finally they came to the day when they were able to nail Him to a cross. That death merely proved the truth of what He had said. At the best, the righteousness of man is as filthy rags in God's sight (see Isa. 64:6). At the worst, man is ready to murder God. Truly, except man's righteousness shall exceed anything that he has yet imagined he shall in no case enter the Kingdom of Heaven.

But the day came when the Lord Jesus poured out His blood in death. He paid the penalty for all the sin of all men. Now men can come and put their trust in Him. Immediately, God places to their account the righteousness of Christ. Now we can enter the Kingdom of Heaven, for, possessing the righteousness of Christ as a gift, we have a righteousness that exceeds the righteousness of the scribes and the Pharisees even as the heavens are higher than the earth.

3

Is the Sermon on the Mount for Today?

The truths taught in the Sermon on the Mount are the righteous foundation of all God's dealings with men. He demands absolute perfection. After the Jews had rejected this foundation the Lord Jesus showed how this righteousness must come as a gift from Himself, since no man has that righteousness in himself. But God has made it possible in the death of Jesus Christ for us to have the righteousness of Christ placed to our account, so that we stand in the sight of God, justified.

This statement concerning the Sermon on the Mount naturally raises certain problems that must be considered. In this present chapter we shall demonstrate from the Bible and from experience that it is impossible to apply without reserve the truths found in the Sermon on the Mount to life as it is in the world today. We shall see that no one living is ever attempting to fulfill all the commands that are laid down in that great discourse. We shall see also that it will take something far greater than the preaching of the Sermon on the Mount, with its golden rule, to right the wrongs that exist in our civilization, and we shall see, finally, what the attitude of the Bible Christian must be toward this great ethical statement of our Lord Jesus.

First of all, is there anyone in the world who is even attempting to live up to all the teachings of the Sermon on the Mount? We are not asking if there are those who honestly try, but fail; rather we are asking if there are any who honestly try. We confess, very frankly, that there are things which are commanded in the Sermon on the Mount which we do not consider as we seek to order our life, even though we are earnestly trying to order all things after the Word of God. The reason we discard such commands is the same reason for which we do not get a lamb and have it killed on an altar by a priest, as was commanded in the Old Testament. All such passages which concern the ceremonialism of the law are, as everyone understands, completely fulfilled by the death of Christ, and we are, henceforth, free from their demands.

In precisely the same way, we are collectively free from certain passages in the Sermon on the Mount because the day of their application has not yet come to the earth, and any attempt to force their application on our present day civilization must end in utter confusion. Later we shall see the application of these verses to individual believers.

Christ always fought against Satan and took care to denounce the children of the devil in no uncertain terms. Jesus Himself protested against being smitten on the cheek when one of the officers of the high priest struck Him (see John 18:23). There is for us, therefore, this example of our Lord, which demonstrates that at one time in His own life He did not "turn the other cheek." Is this not a perfect illustration of the fact that the first phase of His ministry and the last phase differed sharply and He Himself did not follow to the letter the commands of the earlier day, simply because it was not the moment for their detailed application?

The commentators have struggled over the verse ordaining no resistance to evil (see Matt. 5:39) because the masculine and the neuter are the same in the original, and it cannot be certain whether the command is against resistance of the evil one or the evil deed. In either case, we are most certainly to resist in this day and age. "Submit yourself therefore to God. Resist the devil and he will flee from you" (James 4:7). These are our orders for today. Those who attempt to build pacifism on the Sermon on the Mount cannot justify their position. The day of non–resistance will come, but Christ will be back first to establish His rule in such a way that any departure from it shall be immediately judged. To attempt to put all of these precepts into literal fulfillment in our day will be as impossible as any attempt to cause the sun to shine by night.

In fact, we have a remarkable parallel if we consider some of the prophecies that are to be found in the Old Testament concerning certain conditions that are to exist upon this earth one day. Isaiah gives us a delightful picture of life among the animals at the time our Lord shall have established His kingdom upon the earth:

> The wolf also shall dwell with the lamb, and the leopard shall lie down with the kid; and the calf and the young lion and the fatling together; and a little child shall lead them. And the cow and the bear shall feed; their young ones shall lie down together; and the lion shall eat straw like the ox. And the sucking child shall play on the hole of the asp, and the weaned child shall put his hand on the cockatrice' den. They shall not hurt nor destroy in all my holy mountain: for the earth shall be full of the knowledge of the LORD, as the waters cover the sea (Isa. 11:6-9).

This is surely a beautiful picture! Suppose some of our ministers who wish to force the Sermon on the Mount into that place which can be occupied only by the death of our Lord should attempt to bring this vision to fulfillment. Let them take the prophecy of Isaiah to the zoological garden and begin to read this proclamation to the animals in the cages. Will the serpents stop their poisonous biting? Will the lion change over from meat to straw for his food? Will the little child dare to enter the cages of the wild beasts? It will take the miracle of the presence of the returned Son of God to change the face of nature as it shall one day be changed. It will take the same miracle before the picture in the Sermon on the Mount can be realized.

It was with perfect consciousness of this change that the Lord sent forth His disciples with His final counsel to them on the evening before His death. He said to them, "When I sent you without purse, and scrip, and shoes, lacked ye any thing? And they said, Nothing. Then said he unto them, But now, he that hath a purse, let him take it, and likewise his scrip: and he that hath no sword, let him sell his garment, and buy one" (Luke 22:35-36). The reason the Lord Jesus gives for His reversal of orders concerning provision for their needs is that He is about to die. It is His death which fixed the boundary between the test of law to which our Lord had put His people and the test of grace under which we are yet living.

The offer of the Kingdom as made in the Sermon on the Mount is now definitely past. The age of grace runs its course. We are not to make the mistake of trying to force the Sermon on the Mount to a literal fulfillment today. It will be fulfilled literally, but not until the age in which we live has come to its close and the Lord Jesus shall be dealing once more with His people Israel. It is quite clear, therefore, that the Word of God itself shows us that the Sermon on the Mount cannot be forced literally into the individual life. We shall see, further, that it cannot be forced into business life.

In our dealings with men, we associate with a vast number of people who have never accepted the Lord Jesus Christ as their personal Savior. How would it be possible for us to live with them on the basis of a spiritual rule of life of which they can know nothing?

Suppose you turned the other cheek every time someone struck you in some business deal. How long could a Christian last in business with a literal fulfilling of the following verse from the Sermon on the Mount: "And if any man will sue thee at the law, and take away thy coat, let him have thy cloak also" (Matt. 5:40)? The newspapers recently carried a story of a clever lawyer in New York. He made it his sole business to study the charters of corporations, find some tiny flaw, and then buy a few shares of the stock in the market so that he could bring suit as a stockholder against the company in which he had a few hundred dollars equity. The companies found it more profitable to buy him off with a few thousand dollars than to go to court to defend the suit. With such scoundrels alive, what chance would a man have to retain anything if he submitted, passively, to each one who attempted to prey upon him?

It must be stated, however, that the epistles give definite commands to those who are believers not to go to law with each other before unbelievers, but to settle their differences as among Christians and by Christians. The sixth chapter of First Corinthians lays down the principle that we are rather to suffer wrong and be defrauded than to sue a believer. No such restriction is made concerning our dealings with unbelievers.

We have a most interesting incident that took place during the last part of the nineteenth century, which illustrates, in a striking way, the utter impossibility of forcing the Sermon on the Mount upon an unregenerate world at the present time. Tolstoy was one of the greatest writers that Russia ever produced. Unfortunately, he got hold of a New Testament and began to read it. Or rather, we might say, unfortunately, he read only the first few chapters. He was so thrilled with the Sermon on the Mount that the whole of his life and writings were, thenceforth, colored by his reading of it. A little knowledge is a dangerous thing, and when it is a little knowledge of the Bible it becomes even more dangerous than a little knowledge of explosive chemicals might be.

Tolstoy had many influential friends, so when he got an idea he was able to find backing for it. He conceived the project of buying a great stretch of land on the steppes of Russia and colonizing it with men and women who would put the Sermon on the Mount into daily application. They would live together in that state of holy communism, which he imagined was pictured in the Bible, and together, they would demonstrate (on a small scale) what might be possible for the world at large.

But Tolstoy reckoned without the peasants who dwelt outside his colony, in utter ignorance of his high desires. For when several hundred thousand acres of land were secured and peopled with a group of impractical idealists like himself, it was not long before they had lost everything they had. When a neighboring peasant found a stray horse, he took it home to his barn and said nothing about it. When he discovered that no one from the colony made any attempt to secure the return of the horse, he naturally decided that he should go over some evening after dark and get a wagon to go with the horse. Still there was no hue and cry. So, on another night, there was a further excursion to find something that could be put in the wagon. But then he was imprudent enough to tell some of the other peasants about his wonderful discovery and soon they were all trying it for themselves. Tolstoy's colony left the land and returned to the cities, sadder but wiser men. They still had their coats, but they had lost everything else.

Exactly the same result could be obtained in America. Indeed, one of the contributing causes of the financial crash in 1929 was the fact that international bankers sold bonds of foreign powers to the American public when it was definitely known by these same bankers that the bonds were or soon would be worthless, as testimony before the United States Senate committee has proved. Imagine putting the Sermon on the Mount to work with that crowd of thieves! "And if any man...take away thy coat, let him have thy cloak also..." Anyone who knows the slang phrase that is used in Wall Street to describe the condition of the man who has lost in the market, knows that they do not stop with the cloak and the coat.

You might extend this analogy to any phase of life in any country of the world and the results would be exactly the same. There are individuals in the midst of the mass who have personal standards that rise above the average, but the whole current is a swirling torrent that is sucked onward in its flow by the power of selfishness—a force stronger than gravity. The Lord Jesus Himself used force against the money-changers, driving them from the temple, turning over their tables and speaking to them in judgment when He was consumed by the zeal of the Father's house. Why did He not practice what He preached? There is no contradiction when we understand the dispensational position of the Sermon on the Mount.

Then let us turn to the field of government. Do you think that the Sermon on the Mount could be applied to politics today? Will you try it on Tammany Hall? Or can it be made to function in Moscow? Berlin? Rome? Will any one dare have the pride of effrontery and suggest that it could not succeed in these conditions but that it could be brought to work in Washington or London? Every one who follows the Word of God knows that the biblical symbol for government is a wild beast. All shall disappear before the perfect government of our coming Lord. And while we wait, only the born again man can even approach the fringe of the possibilities of the Sermon on the Mount.

Would you apply the Sermon on the Mount to our social system? There are more slaves in the world today than there were when Jesus Christ was on earth. There is one difference, however, between that day and this. When men bought slaves on the block they cared for them at least as well as they did for their cattle. To lose a good slave was to lose real money. In our time, however, the slaves are paid by the day and forced to take care of themselves. When Sherman marched from Atlanta to the sea, he laid waste a land whose masters took the shreds that were left and shared them with their slaves. But when depression marches from sea to sea, the first thought of the masters is to cut loose the slaves and leave them helpless before charity.

A well–known liberal minister said recently,

As things are now, we cannot love our neighbours as ourselves… Although today there is more than enough bread to go around, it is not going around and, apparently, cannot be made to go around in the economic system which we now have—a fact which condemns our present system far more severely than do the bitterest words of its bitterest critics. Thou shalt love thy neighbour as thyself: that, according to Jesus and according to history!—is one of the most important and imperative words that ever proceeded out of the mouth of God. And today we cannot obey it, even those of us who are eager to do so. We find ourselves entrapped in a system that makes it impossible for us to obey it. But obey it we must. My own conviction is that obedience means recovery, and that disobedience means revolution.

The second commandment, then, is this: Thou shalt build an economic system and a social order in which it shall be possible for people to love their neighbours as themselves.

What a confession! But this man, evidently blind to the real truth of God's Word, thinks that man himself can bring in this miracle change.

Common sense tells us that the world is, indeed, out of order. The Sermon on the Mount does not fit into any phase of our civilization. This puts a definite question before those of us who believe that the Bible is the inspired Word of God. When will the Sermon on the Mount become effective? The answer is not hard to find. It will take the personal return of the Lord Jesus Christ, coming not as the meek and lowly Savior, but as the Lord of power and glory, to enforce righteous principles upon this earth. The earth will have Him as Dictator soon, and He will see to it that the pure in heart see God, that the poor in spirit shall enter the Kingdom of Heaven, that the mourners shall be comforted, that the meek shall inherit the earth.

James, the brother of our Lord, was used by the Holy Spirit to write down that great prophecy concerning the rich men who had heaped their treasures together for the last days. First, he cried out, "Behold, the hire of the labourers who have reaped down your fields, which is of you kept back by fraud, crieth: and the cries of them which have reaped are entered into the ears of the Lord of sabaoth" (James 5:4). Then he added, "Be patient therefore, brethren, unto the coming of the Lord" (James 5:7). This is that for which we wait.

The Lord Jesus will soon lay aside the robes of His mediation and come forth to rule and to reign. He shall dash His enemies to pieces like a potter's vessel, and shall rule with a rod of iron (see Ps. 2:9). David drew a prophetic picture of His reign when he said,

He shall judge thy people with righteousness, and thy poor with judgment… He shall judge the poor of the people, he shall save the children of the needy, and shall break in pieces the oppressor… He shall come down like rain upon the mown grass: as showers that water the earth. In his days shall the righteous flourish; and abundance of peace so long as the moon endureth (Ps. 72:2, 4, 6-7).

When He is reigning upon the earth it will be right to turn the other cheek. It will be right to follow a policy of pacifism before an unregenerate world. For in that day when the evil and selfish instincts of men break out against their neighbors, the one who is oppressed will be sure, in submitting, that in a flash some mighty angel will be there taking vengeance. When our Lord shall rule, righteousness shall dominate, no false witness will be possible and there will be no technicalities in His law through which the guilty may escape.

There is one more phase of our problem that we must consider. We have seen that the Sermon on the Mount is primarily for the future. During the years of the reign of the Antichrist, God's own upon the earth will be pleading the clauses of these great pictures of promise. Moreover, with the coming of the Lord Jesus Christ to the earth, these principles shall come into effect as a constitution that shall never need an amendment.

The question that we must ask ourselves is that which concerns our present individual attitude toward the principles that are laid down in the Sermon on the Mount. Does a believer in Christ have the right to be proud and arrogant simply because it is demonstrated that the literal inheritance of the meek is future? The mere statement of the question is a sufficient refutation.

The detailed rule of the life of the believer is to be found in the epistles that were addressed to the churches. Here we find the high and exalted position that is ours today. We find more than a code of commandments, more than a set of conditions. We discover that God is providing us with a miraculous life. He tells us that when we accept the Lord Jesus Christ as our personal Savior, we are the objects of a work that is a new creation. We receive a new nature. We are able to say, "I am crucified with Christ: nevertheless I live; yet not I, but Christ liveth in me: and the life which I now live in the flesh I live by the faith of the Son of God, who loved me, and gave himself for me" (Gal. 2:20).

We find that many of the principles expressed in the Sermon on the Mount are repeated in no uncertain terms for the daily walk of the believer. Are not all the implications of the beatitudes summed up in that great promise made to the Galatian church? "But the fruit of the Spirit is love, joy, peace, patience, kindness, goodness, faithfulness, gentleness, self-control; against such there is no law" (Gal. 5:22-23 RSV). All the comfort that is to be found in the promises concerning the lilies of the field and the birds of the air is to be found in the repeated promises which are made to us. In fact, the repetition of these promises is made in a form that is much more sure and strong. "He that spared not his own Son, but delivered him up for us all, how shall he not with him also freely give us all things?" (Rom. 8:32). This is a promise that is based on the covenant of blood, while the same promises as found in the Sermon on the Mount are based more on that which man is doing.

There is one principle in the Sermon on the Mount which is reversed for us in the epistles. It is a clause that is found in the so-called Lord's Prayer. There we read, in the language of the King James translation, "And forgive us our debts, as we forgive our debtors" (Matt. 6:12). If we quote the Church of England prayer book version, we have that which is taken from an older translation, "Forgive us our trespasses, as we forgive them who trespass against us."

Did you ever stop to analyze that statement without prejudice? What are you praying when you say that clause? You are asking God for an imperfect forgiveness. You are asking Him to make the forgiveness that comes from your sinful heart the basis of His forgiveness. Think of it! If a bankrupt who owed everybody and could pay nothing, should go to the man who owed him a great sum and say, "Please pay me, on the same ratio that I am paying everyone whom I owe," he would soon learn the folly of his asking. But turn to the last verse in the fourth chapter of Ephesians. Here we read, "And be ye kind one to another, tenderhearted, forgiving one another, even as God for Christ's sake hath forgiven you" (Eph. 4:32).

When I read this, I know I have arrived at home. This is the kind of prayer I can pray. It will rise from a thankful heart that feels and knows the grace of God. It will be a prayer which says, "May I be able to forgive those who trespass against me with that same forgiveness that Thou hast bestowed when Thou didst take my sins and remove them as far as the east is from the west, and when Thou didst say that Thou wouldst remember them against me no more, forever." That is a prayer that my renewed heart can understand. But in the days when He spoke, when law yet reigned, and grace had not come into effect, there could be no such full forgiveness from God.

The attitude of the true believer in Christ is not that of wondering how little he must do to satisfy God, but that of eager desire to fulfill all that is possible. His is the attitude that desires to find out about the known and the unknown will of God. One autumn, as the holiday season was approaching, my sisters and I talked together about what Christmas present we could get for our mother, who is now in Heaven. She was a very wonderful woman, and her wants were very few. So we listened and watched her every word. Finally, she mentioned a certain article, quite casually, and we never gave any sign that we had noticed it. A month or so went by before Christmas came, but when the packages were opened we saw the delighted surprise on the face of our mother as she exclaimed, "Oh, how did you know that I wanted that? I have wanted it so much." And we were more than repaid, for our love had gone out of the way to surprise her desire and to fulfill it.

The one who has been born again will learn to love our Lord because He first loved us. We will study His Word, not with any thought of fear, but because we love our Lord and wish to know His will. And if we can find in some passage like the Sermon on the Mount a picture of that which He will fulfill upon the earth when He comes to reign, our eager hearts will turn to Him and say, " Lord, this may not be for the time in which the world agonizes in its bitter pain today. But Lord, here is Thy redeemed child. I desire Thy will, all Thy will that I can know. Do in me as Thou dost desire." And there will be the delight of fellowship between us as we turn to that Sermon on the Mount which shall find its world-wide fulfillment in the future, and as we say to Him, "Thy will be done"—IN ME—"as it is in heaven."

In that day, the true and yielded believer will delight at every possibility of present-day fulfillment in our hearts, for we have been begotten from the dead in order "that we should be a kind of firstfruits of his creatures" that one day shall dominate the earth (see James 1:18).

4
CHRIST AND THE LAW

When the Lord Jesus Christ began His ministry, He ran counter to the preconceived notions of the religious leaders of His day. These men were living under the law of Moses, but they had so encrusted that law with their own ideas and explanations that it was no longer the same as that which God gave His people. The law is "holy, and just, and good" (Rom. 7:12), but these religious leaders were unholy, unjust and evil.

As soon as Christ began His ministry, these leaders began to measure Him and His sayings by means of the standard which they thought was God's law. But their measure was absolutely false. Lord Kelvin, late head of the British Scientific Association, said that no man truly knew anything that he could not measure. If this be true, it is certain that the leaders in Israel knew nothing about God, for they had broken His law by the simple expedient of taking His divine measure, the law, and altering it to fit their desires.

John E. Sears, leading British authority on metrology, speaking before the Royal Institute in 1926, said that the standard yard of Queen Elizabeth in the sixteenth century was still in use as a standard as late as 1824, although in the interval it had been broken and "crudely repaired by dowelling and binding the two pieces together with two strips of sheet brass and copper wire." This is indeed enough to make any self–respecting scientist's hair turn!

But the breaking of God's standard by the Pharisees in the time of Christ was not even an honest accident. It was not that the law of God had been altered and that they had done their best to repair that standard. It would appear, on the other hand, both from the teaching of Christ and from our knowledge of the literature of the Talmud, that these men had deliberately whittled down the standard which God had given in order that it might fit, more closely, that which they knew to be their own measurements.

No wonder, therefore, that the preaching of Christ, with His standard of perfect righteousness, put these gentlemen into such a fit of consternation! Immediately they wanted to know the attitude of Christ toward the law. They were thinking, of course, of what they imagined the law to be. He, naturally, answered in terms of the law of Moses, just as God had given it, without lowering its stupendous claims against the individual.

Men of our day have much to say concerning Christ and the Old Testament. It is quite common to hear, or to read, that men of this enlightened twentieth century wish to follow the religion of Jesus. They, because of their superior intellect and greater insight into spiritual matters, so they say, do not wish to have anything to do with the Old Testament. There are those who claim even to see a difference between the Jehovah of the Old Testament and the God of the New. They look at Christ's statements in the Sermon on the Mount and then begin to talk about the horrid conception of God that they claim is found in the Old Testament. They call Him a tribal God and proceed to thank their god that they have been removed from a thought of God that is so unrefined and barbarous as to desire a blood sacrifice. They flee from a God who would punish a people by death for such minor offenses as complaining against Moses or hiding away their loot in a tent. Yet they are incapable of comprehending the fact that Jesus Christ associated Himself with the God of the Old Testament and with the Old Testament itself in such a way as to render the Book and the person of God and Christ absolutely inseparable.

It is not our purpose here to make a study of the great subjects that are involved in such a question. Suffice it to say that any logical mind must be forced to the conclusion that the God of Jesus Christ was the God of the Old Testament and that Christ Himself accepted the Scriptures as the very Word of God. The difficulties which some men seem to find in accepting our Lord Jehovah, as He is revealed throughout the Bible, do not arise from the facts that are to be found concerning Him, but from the blindness of men's sinful hearts. They fail to see either the wonderful holiness of God or the intrinsic sinfulness of sin. When men catch a glimpse of what sin really is and then consider it against the background of the holiness of God, every problem is resolved and the difficulties fade away.

The whole of the ministry of the Lord Jesus Christ—whether that first part in which He offered the Kingdom to Israel, or the latter part in which He prepared to face the cross in order that He might become the Redeemer of Jew or Gentile alike—was enacted against the background of the Jewish law. We speak of it as the Jewish law, although, more correctly, it must be called the law of the Lord Jehovah, as given through His servant Moses to the children of Israel.

In the first place, Jesus Christ was born, humanly speaking, subject to that law. We read in the Epistle to the Galatians, "But when the fulness of the time was come, God sent forth his Son, made of a woman, made under the law, To redeem them that were under the law, that we might receive the adoption of sons" (Gal. 4:4-5). We see here, of course, the dual nature of our Lord, Who was both the eternal Son, sent forth, and the human child, born. But the point we wish to make here is that God says that Christ was "made of a woman, made under the law." That He was "made under the law," means that He was subject to all the laws and ordinances of the Old Testament. We might even say that He was subject to all the laws and ordinances of the Jews, but this would be inexact since they had altered the biblical law and added to it and taken from it to such an extent that it was necessary for Christ to fight the leaders on the grounds of the law at almost every step of His way.

Christ was subject to the Old Testament law in so far as His human nature was concerned. This is the reason why He accepted baptism from John. That rite was administered to others as a sign of repentance and remission of sins. Christ had nothing of which to repent and no sins that needed pardon. Yet He answered, when John protested against performing the ceremony, "Suffer it to be so now: for thus it becometh us to fulfil all righteousness" (Matt. 3:15). Some have wondered why, indeed, Jesus Christ should have submitted Himself to this rite which signified confession and repentance. But it seems evident that the answer lies in the fact that the Lord Jesus Christ was then about to begin the long, hard, three years' journey of submission to every law and ordinance and rite of His people, and so He allowed John the Baptist to lay his hands upon Him. It is, perhaps, worth pointing out that here is the fulfillment of the type of the scapegoat. John laid his hands upon the head of our Lord, as the priest laid his hands on the head of the scapegoat, and, "Then was Jesus led up of the Spirit into the wilderness…" (Matt. 4:1).

The law of the sacrifices demanded that the lamb offered upon the altar should be a firstling of the flock, without spot or blemish. The Lord Jesus Christ was indeed the firstborn of all creation, but it was by His submission to the law in its every detail that Jesus Christ became eligible to die as the Lamb of God which taketh away the sin of the world.

This is evident at the outset of His public work by reason of His answer to Satan when the prince of this world came with the first temptation. Christ had spent forty days in the wilderness, fasting, and He was hungry. Satan came and tempted Him to use His divine nature to help out His human nature. "If thou be the Son of God, command that these stones be made bread" (Matt. 4:3). When Satan said, "If thou be the Son of God," there was certainly no doubt expressed. We must not forget that our word "if" has two entirely different meanings. In a home there may be a young man in whose word no one has much confidence. He starts to leave the house and upon being asked where he is going, replies evasively that he is just going down to the store. Someone may answer, "Well, if you are going to the store, I am astonished." This expresses doubt. But a while later, the mother in the home starts toward the door. The same question is asked and the same answer is received. She is going to the store. "Oh," says some member of the family, "if you are going to the store will you ask for the package I left there." This "if" is one of absolute certainty. It means "because." "Because you are going to the store, bring me my package."

In exactly the same way Satan approached our Lord. The temptation of our Lord might be paraphrased as follows: "You have the very nature of God, which you received from Your Father. Use this nature and its power to help out the poor hungering body of Your human nature. You have the power to turn these stones into bread because You are the Son of God. Use that power to live a comfortable life." With His very first word the Lord Jesus answered the tempter. "Man shall not live by bread alone, but by every word that proceedeth out of the mouth of God" (Matt. 4:4). If we were to paraphrase this answer it would be as follows: "No. I will not use the divine nature to come to the aid of the human nature. It is as a man that I am going to meet these temptations and overcome them."

In other words, the power that issued in the holy life of the Lord Jesus Christ was not the arbitrary choice of the divine nature of our Lord. And we see why this must be, for, in all reverence, we may say that any of us could live a life as holy as that of the Lord Jesus if we had only a divine nature with which to live it. But the Lord Jesus Christ lived on earth as a man. It was a life that was lived in a power which did not find its first impulsion in the divine nature of the Son of God. It was a life lived as a man depending upon the divine nature. It was a momentary, constant dependence upon the God-nature.

In this way the manhood of our Lord Jesus becomes a perfect example for us. We, too, may live in constant dependence upon our Lord. If we do not, we are doomed to failure. True victory over sin can come only from that gaze fixed upon our Lord, which keeps us constantly yielded to His will. So, as a man, our Lord Jesus Christ overcame the tempter, and thus the firstborn was without spot or blemish, and might rightfully go to the cross and die in our place.

This leads us on to the study of a most important declaration of our Lord concerning His relationship to the law. In the midst of the Sermon on the Mount He said, "Think not that I am come to destroy the law, or the prophets: I am not come to destroy, but to fulfil" (Matt. 5:17). And He then added that great promise and prophecy concerning the stability of this Word of God's revelation to us, "For verily I say unto you, Till heaven and earth pass, one jot or one tittle shall in no wise pass from the law till all be fulfilled" (Matt. 5:18).

Some have drawn from this statement the absurd conclusion that the believer of our day is obligated to keep the law in order to be saved. We must not forget that the law is not merely the code which we know as the Ten Commandments, but that it includes all the ordinances for life and living which were given by God through Moses and which constitute the whole of the priestly code. Christ came to fulfill it all. No one who lived before that moment had ever fulfilled the law. Therefore, everyone who lived under the law was under the curse which was necessarily attached to the breaking of the law.

Mark well: no one who lived before Christ came had kept the law. Therefore everyone came under the curse. This was true of Moses, Joshua, David, Solomon, Elijah, Elisha, and all the mighty men of the old dispensation. God knew when He gave the law that no one would ever be able to fulfill it, and so He provided a lamb at the same time that He gave the law. When the law was broken, the lamb was to be sacrificed. This was not a provision given in order to make sinning easy, but an imperious necessity from the heart of a loving God, because He knew that His holiness demanded a perfection as expressed in the law, which no man could fulfill.

So there was to be salvation through faith in God's Word about the blood of a sacrifice. This was because God had in His plan that Man Christ Jesus Who was to come and fulfill the law. As soon as Christ had lived His perfect life, the law was fulfilled. It could have no further hold on those who would believe in the Lord's sacrificial work.

There is a partial analogy in one of the well–known scenes from Greek mythology. Near the town of Thebes, legend says, there existed a monster, the sphinx, who proposed a riddle to every passerby and devoured those who were unable to solve it. Oedipus came and fulfilled the condition, thereby destroying the power of the monster over Thebes, and thus he came to the throne of the city. This analogy is only partial because the law is not a monster, but the law is "holy, and just, and good." But it had its hold over men and its curse upon them because it was the very embodiment of the absolute holiness of God.

This is the great principle which is laid down throughout the Bible: there will be no one in Heaven unless he is as holy as God, as perfect as the law, as righteous as the Lord Jesus Christ. Anyone who cannot live up to these demands must take his place as a lost sinner. This was the curse of the law. Christ came and fulfilled the law, took the curse upon Himself, so that those who believe in Him may know that this curse is gone forever. For in dying on the cross, Christ provided a perfect righteousness which may be written down to our account in that perfect transaction. When we have accepted that gift by faith, we stand before God, credited with a righteousness which is not our own, but which is wholly satisfactory to God, and fulfills all His claims against us. Perhaps the most important statement that could be made concerning the death of Jesus Christ is that God is satisfied with Christ's death in place of that of the sinner. This is the heart message of Christianity. Nothing else is Christianity.

But let us note this further detail concerning our Lord and the law. Not only did He make this definite prophecy concerning His purpose with regard to the fulfillment of the law (which purpose He accomplished on Calvary), but He proceeded to set the leaders of the people right concerning the spiritual nature of the law. In their minds, a man was not a murderer until the last gasp of the breath of life had left the body of the victim. Christ pointed out that hatred in the heart was as much murder as the overt drama. They had considered adultery only as a physical act. The Lord Jesus placed the guilt in the realm of thought. To think sin is to be guilty of it. This was a transgression of the perfect law of God as well as the flagrant act. Not only was there this great call to the spiritual understanding of the law, but also there was the amplifying of the law.

The Man Who stood on the mount to preach His sermon was none other than the God Who had stood on Mount Sinai to give the law through Moses. Now He had come to fulfill it. This was done not only through His matchless life furnishing the accomplishment of all its demands, but also through the full flowering of its meaning. Nine times there is the great statement, "I say unto you" (Matt. 5). This is the God of the heavens Who speaks from the mountain. He was fulfilling the law; that is, He was bringing it to its full development.

The French Catholic commentator, M. Auguste Crampon, writes on this verse,

> Jesus brought to realization in His person all the types and prophecies. When He tore away from the law the human interpretations which altered its spiritual intent, He brought it back to its divine ideal: thus the new covenant will be established upon the old as upon a divinely prepared foundation, just as the fruit will follow the flower quite naturally, without there being any destruction or overthrow, but rather by blossoming and development (note on Matthew 5:17).

Nevertheless, there are people who, in their blindness, claim that the Sermon on the Mount is their creed. Far from this, however, this sermon is really that which condemns them even more than the law of the Old Testament. It is the declaration that transgression comes from the heart and that the heart is evil and corrupt. This is the verdict of God which declares man's lost condition.

This is the reason why it is necessary to be born again. There is nothing in any man which could give him strength to live up to the code given by God through Moses; how much more, then, must we realize that there is nothing in man which could give him strength to live up to the even more impossible code which is given by Christ? We are forced away from any thought of salvation by character. We must flee to the cross where the blood of Jesus Christ cleanses from all sin, and where His righteousness, the righteousness of Christ within us, can be placed to our account.

It is in this provision that we see the highest purpose which God has expressed concerning Christ and the law. We have seen, first, that the law is "holy, and just, and good." It can never be anything else, since God gave it to men as a standard. It is an expression of His perfection, and shows us that He must demand perfection of men. Secondly, we have seen that Christ accomplished all the law in Himself, fulfilling every detail of it in His own human perfection, yielded and dependent upon the power of God. He amplified it by giving to it an even stronger hold upon man and increasing its demands. Consequently, He showed the sinfulness of man against a sharper background of light. Then, having lived His life of perfection, He could go to the cross and die, and thus redeem us from the curse of the law. How was this accomplished?

He did not destroy the law, for the law is perfect. The law remains, but He takes all those who believe in His substitutionary death out from under the demands of the law, in order that they might be submitted to the even higher law of His love and grace. When men desire to have a case at law taken from one locality to another or from the jurisdiction of one court to that of another, they may do so under established legal procedure. This "change of venue" is expressed in a great passage in the Epistle to the Romans. "Wherefore, my brethren, ye also are become dead to the law by the body of Christ; that ye should be married to another, even to him who is raised from the dead, that we should bring forth fruit unto God" (Rom. 7:4).

This is the great result of the death of Jesus Christ. Those who believe in Him are no longer under the necessary wrath of God, which must break forth wherever that perfect law is violated in thought, word, or deed. Such violation deserves Hell, but Christ took our Hell and there can be nothing left for us but His Heaven. Henceforth there is no court in the universe that will receive a charge against God's elect, or sit in judgment upon the one whom Christ has freed.

But this freedom from the penalty of the law does not remove us from the obligation of holiness. The work of Christ takes us out from under the curse of the law but it also plants within us a new life that makes it possible for the holiness which the law demands to be brought into our lives. In the eighth chapter of Romans there is a final statement concerning Christ and the law where we read, "There is therefore now no condemnation to them which are in Christ Jesus" (Rom. 8:1). This is the freedom from the penalty of the law of which we have just spoken. The passage then goes on to explain this freedom which believers know. "For the law of the Spirit of life in Christ Jesus hath made me free from the law of sin and death. For what the law could not do, in that it was weak through the flesh, God sending his own Son in the likeness of sinful flesh, and for sin, condemned sin in the flesh: That the righteousness of the law might be fulfilled in us, who walk not after the flesh, but after the Spirit" (Rom. 8:2-4). We now are able to see the perfect working out of God's plan and the place of the law in that plan.

Man had sinned, but was not willing to admit his lost condition. God gave the law from Mount Sinai, amplifying it in the Sermon on the Mount, which shows the perfection of His demands. The sinfulness of man makes it impossible that any individual should ever live up to these demands. God knew this in advance, and His purpose in giving the law was to bring man to a sense of his need that he might abandon the way of self-effort and turn to God's grace. Christ came and died on the cross, taking the stroke of God's justice, thus condemning the sinfulness of man and paying the penalty. Now, the risen Lord Jesus Christ can come dwell in the life of the man who accepts Him as Savior. He is able to accomplish within us that holiness which the law demanded but which the flesh was never able to attain. In the measure that we yield to this new life of Christ, the new law operates, the law of the Spirit of life of the risen Christ, and makes it possible for God to bring righteousness to fruition in our daily lives.

52

5
CHRIST'S GREAT CRISIS

There is no doubting the fact that there are seeming contradictions in the Bible. But to anyone who has studied the laws of evidence, it is a simple matter to determine the fact that these contradictions are on the surface only, while down underneath there is a harmony so wonderful that the divinity of this Book cannot be questioned. If men get together in a lawyer's office and plan what testimony shall be given in order to hide the truth, their testimony will seem to be in accord. There will be no surface contradictions. But a good trial lawyer will pierce this placid surface and reach down to the muddy slime that lies underneath.

On the other hand, where there is truth, there may be contradictions upon the surface, for life is infinitely varied, but there will be full agreement down underneath. One statement will harmonize two others which have seemed in contradiction. It is so with the Bible. A statement in one of the Gospels will often bring full harmony to a story whose details seem to diverge in two other Gospels. There is the added testimony of truth unto itself.

The verse in John that we are considering unlocks more closed doors than any other key in the New Testament. Here we have the interpretation of the whole of the life of Christ. "He came unto his own, and his own received him not. But as many as received him, to them gave he power to become the sons of God, even to them that believe on his name." This word "but" is like a watershed that divides a continent.

Why, then, is it that men cannot see this simple fact? They understand it in relationship to modern historical figures. Any writer discussing the life of George Washington would have to consider the great differences animating all his actions from the moment he cast his lot with the Revolution. This transition period took him out of the role of private citizen and placed him in the spotlight of the most publicized position in the country. It is just as possible for us to trace the steps in the recorded history of the life of the Lord Jesus Christ which changed His ministry from that of the national Messiah, presenting His claims only to Israel, to that of the world-Savior, offering Heaven to each individual of the race who is willing to accept Him as sacrificial substitute.

It was necessary that He should come first of all to the Jews. God had bound Himself by His given Word, and that covenant promise had to be fulfilled. So He came unto His own, and offered them the Kingdom in righteousness. This they refused. Then there was a right–about–face movement which set Him on the path that took Him, ultimately, to the cross.

One event in the life of our Lord gives us the background for this great change in His ministry. It is the imprisonment of John the Baptist and the incident that grew out of the message sent by the prisoner to the Lord Jesus Christ. John had announced the necessity of repentance and of a return to righteousness on the part of the leaders. Their unregenerate hearts could do nothing but hate him for it. Ultimately his preaching displeased the governor, and John was cast into prison. Our Lord knew that His own preaching must have the same type of reception from that godless generation, but He went quietly about His work, preaching, teaching, and working miracles.

John the Baptist was a human being, subject to all the weaknesses which mankind knows. Even the bravest men, when confined to a dungeon, must be influenced somewhat by the dim light which filters in through iron bars. John the Baptist had preached a message that referred to the Kingdom work of Christ. His preaching had all been occupied with the Messiah Who was to come in judgment and break the yoke of the enemy. John, most probably, had thought that he himself would be given some honorable place in that new government in view of his faithfulness as the forerunner. He had been a voice, crying in the wilderness. His natural mind must have desired a part in the breaking of the yoke of the enemy or, at least, a portion in the government which should be set up in righteousness. The Spirit came upon him at the time of the baptism of Jesus and he cried, "Behold the Lamb of God, which taketh away the sin of the world" (John 1:29), but he did not understand all that he was saying. Events demonstrate that he had hope, even after he was in prison, that the earthly Kingdom might soon be set up.

The eleventh chapter of Matthew is one of the pivotal passages in the Bible. John the Baptist, from his prison, sent two of his disciples to find Jesus and ask Him a question. They came with John's message, "Art thou he that should come, or do we look for another?" (Matt. 11:3). There is no avoiding the implications of this question. If we paraphrase the thought, it will read: "We have been expecting that Thou wouldst do all that we prophesied of Thee. We said that the Messiah Who was to follow us would come in judgment. His axe would be laid to the root of the trees that did not produce good fruit. His winds of judgment would sweep away the chaff and leave the threshing floor with its cleansed wheat. But now we find ourselves in prison with a sword hanging over us. We had expected that Thou wouldst break forth in Thy judgment work, long before this. Have we misunderstood the Scriptures? Art

Thou He that should come, or look we for another who will complete the work that is prophesied concerning the Messiah and which we had expected of Thee long ere this?"

Jesus answered and said to them, "Go and shew John again those things which ye do hear and see: The blind receive their sight, and the lame walk, the lepers are cleansed, and the deaf hear, the dead are raised up, and the poor have the gospel preached to them" (Matt. 11:4-5). There is nothing new in that answer. Indeed, Jesus said to these disciples, "Go and show John again." Tell him once more. In other words, John already knew that which Jesus was answering through the two disciples. But there was one more phrase in our Lord's answer. It was added, almost as a postscript is added to a letter. We must not forget that the question was asked and the answer given in the midst of a crowd, some of whom would have been only too happy to hear and repeat some word of criticism from the Lord against John. The last line of the message was one that was spoken as apart from the work He had been doing, but uttered to give John the spiritual clue to the understanding of the life and work of the Lord Jesus.

Jesus added this most significant sentence, "And blessed is he, whosoever shall not be offended in me" (Matt. 11:6). This verse is a spiritual touchstone for the estimate of real knowledge of the Bible. The man who cannot see the hidden meaning of this verse is lacking in that insight which is given of the Spirit for the unfolding of the message of the Word of God. There were many people who were offended with Jesus. He was despised and rejected of men. When He went to the cross, He went alone. All His disciples left Him. None of them understood that He was to go to the cross. They all expected Him to manifest Himself as the conquering Messiah. None of them realized that His death would end His physical work on earth for centuries to come. Only Mary of Bethany realized that He was to die. She alone anointed His body for the burial (see John 12:7) and there is no evidence that she was among those who sought Him at the tomb.

When the Lord prophesied His death to His disciples they were confused. We read in the ninth chapter of Mark that Jesus said to His disciples, "The Son of man is delivered into the hands of men, and they shall kill him; and after that he is killed, he shall rise the third day. But they understood not that saying, and were afraid to ask him" (Mark 9:31-32). Christ did all that could be done to teach them. But even on the night before His crucifixion, they did not understand what was about to happen, though He had told them so plainly. He even said, "These things have I spoken unto you, that ye should not be offended" (John 16:1).

But to the two disciples of John, coming with the message from the faithful man in prison, Jesus said, "And blessed is he, whosoever shall not be offended in me." He certainly knew that some would be thus offended. What did He mean? There can be but one answer. He knew that there was confusion in the minds of the disciples concerning the work that He was to do. He knew that they had filled their minds with part of the truth and that that incomplete truth was to become an error in their thinking. We must never forget that incomplete doctrine may become false doctrine. A partial view of the doctrine of the Holy Spirit causes the excesses of Pentecostalism. An incomplete view of prophetic truth brings forth those cults which set dates for the return of Christ. A one-sided view of the teaching of the cross results in modernism and the cults that deny salvation through the blood.

The incomplete truth which was held by John the Baptist and the disciples of the Lord would lead them to become offended with Him. They wanted the work of the second coming before He performed the redemptive work of His first coming. They wanted the Kingdom, but they did not see that it must be founded on righteousness. Since man has no righteousness of His own, the Kingdom must be founded on the righteousness of God. That righteousness cannot be communicated unto man apart from the justifying work of Christ's atoning death. So when Jesus Christ sent back word to John in prison, "And blessed is he, whosoever shall not be offended in me," He was really saying, "Blessed is that man who does not have an incomplete view of truth. Blessed is that man who is not expecting the Kingdom to be accomplished before a basis of righteousness is provided for it. Blessed is the man who does not expect the second coming before the first."

One outstanding incident occurring on the day of the resurrection gives us a perfect view of the mental processes of the disciples. On Easter morning, the risen Lord met two of His own disciples on the road to Emmaus as they were returning home from the Passover. These men were greatly disheartened by the crucifixion scene. So Jesus asked them about their evident sorrow. They explained why they were sad: "Jesus of Nazareth," they said, "had been crucified." Just what did that mean to them, personally? Their answer was a confession: "But we trusted that it had been he which should have redeemed Israel" (Luke 24:21).

They were looking for redemption by power before there was redemption by blood. They had not comprehended the proper sequence. It was as though the children of Israel had expected to pass through the Red Sea and see Pharaoh's army destroyed, before the lamb had been slain, the blood applied to the door, and the angel of death had passed over the homes of Israel while bringing death to Egypt. It was the slain lamb that was to make it possible for Israel to leave their bondage for freedom. Redemption by blood always precedes redemption by power. Christ paid the penalty for our sin before He made it possible for us to have personal victory over sins. These two disciples showed that they were expecting redemption from Roman slavery before there was redemption from sin's dominion.

What did Christ say to these two who had been trusting that He should have redeemed Israel? "Then he said unto them, O fools, and slow of heart to believe all that the prophets have spoken: Ought not Christ to have suffered these things, and to enter into his glory?" (Luke 24:25-26). He rebuked them because their partial view of doctrine had led them into great error. All this truth is indicated in Jesus' great answer to John's disciples "And blessed is he whosoever shall not be offended in me."

After Christ's answer concerning John the Baptist, the messengers went back to John. Jesus turned to the crowd who had undoubtedly listened closely to hear what Jesus would have to say to the disciples of the man who had created such interest in Israel. Multitudes had gone forth to hear him, and "all men mused in their hearts of John, whether he were the Christ, or not" (Luke 3:15). We must not forget that our Lord was a perfect gentleman, and therefore, He would take particular pains to speak well of John. It was like our Lord to give His disciples credit whenever it was possible. Indeed, any credit due us, we have from the wonderful grace of God.

Jesus then began to speak to the crowd about John. He was going to test their hearts. Why had they gone out into the desert after John? Was it to see a reed shaken with the wind? Of course not. Men do not follow weaklings. The man who does not have strength cannot attract a crowd and hold them. This, then, is the admission of John's strength. He was a man of power. But what kind of power did he have? The Lord asked His second question. Why did they go out into the desert? Was it to see a man clothed in soft raiment? Of course not. The Roman world was full of sycophants who had achieved power through flattery or through sin. Weak men could pander to the lusts of strong men and so achieve a certain power that would be supported by the force of Roman arms, but this was not a power that could attract men. The crowd might fawn before this silken–sleek power that was to be found in kings' houses but it would not take the trouble to go out of the city into a desert place in order to gaze upon such men.

But with John the Baptist it was different. Here was virile strength. This man had the stuff of a real leader. But was that all? Jesus went on to His third question. Did you go out into the desert to see a prophet? Yes. John was a prophet, but he was more than a prophet. He was the one of whom the Spirit spoke in the Old Testament when it was written, "Behold, I send my messenger before thy face, which shall prepare thy way before thee" (Matt. 11:10). So John was not only a prophet, but he was the object of prophecy. His work was to be linked inseparably with that of the promised Messiah.

Now Jesus moved on to His final statement concerning John, which is the greatest of all the statements made about him. He said that John the Baptist was greater than all the men who had been born up to that time. "Verily I say unto you, Among them that are born of women there hath not risen a greater than John the Baptist" (Matt. 11:11). John the Baptist, greater than Enoch, Noah, Abraham, Isaac, Jacob, Joseph, Moses, Joshua, Samuel, Elijah, Elisha, David, Solomon, Isaiah, Jeremiah, Daniel and a host of others! It seems almost incredible, but we must get the divine viewpoint. Our Lord said it was true, and that is sufficient.

Christ now proceeds to speak of new things, and new relationships. Even though John was greater than all who had risen before that time, there was to be a new order of events. The least in the Kingdom of Heaven would be greater than John the Baptist.

Some day that Kingdom will be established. The King will come to rule and reign. He will be ruling over the world by means of His glorified saints who shall judge the world. We read in Corinthians, "Do ye not know that the saints shall judge the world?" (1 Cor. 6:2). To the one, our Lord will give one city, to another five cities, to another ten cities. He that has been faithful in few things shall be made ruler over many. Even the least in that day shall be greater than John the Baptist. This is not hard to believe when we realize all the glory of the time when we shall see our Lord and be like Him (see 1 John 3:2); when we shall have resurrection bodies made like unto His glorified body (see Phil. 3:21). What a glorious future is ours in that day!

And now Jesus changed the subject to speak of the imprisonment of John. This led Him to a condemnation of those forces in control which were ultimately to nail Him to the cross of Calvary. Here is the setting of the stage for the events of one of the greatest days in His life, the day in which He broke with the rulers of Israel. He had come unto His own and His own had refused to receive Him. But now He was ready to turn away from them. He made them a bona fide offer of the Kingdom. But from the first announcement made by John the Baptist until the moment He spoke, the leaders had met every presentation of the righteousness of the Kingdom with undisguised violence. Their hearts were filled with hatred. They had put John in prison. He would soon die. The violent were seeking to destroy this Kingdom by force. If these leaders had been willing to repent and accept the principles of righteousness which the Lord announced, He would have counted John the Baptist as the one to do the work prophesied of Elijah in the last two verses of the Old Testament. Later on, the Lord said of John the Baptist, "But I say unto you, That Elias is come already, and they knew him not, but have done unto him whatsoever they listed" (Matt. 17:12).

And now we can see the mounting wrath of God. The meek and lowly Jesus was about to blaze forth against the cities which had rejected His teaching and against the blind leaders of the blind who had now fallen into the ditch of open rejection of the Son of God.

Our Lord paused at this point to give us one vivid, though sorrowful, illustration of the mentality of the people who were rejecting His teaching. He looked out over the people and said, "But whereunto shall I liken this generation? It is like unto children sitting in the markets, and calling unto their fellows, And saying, We have piped unto you and ye have not danced; we have mourned unto you, and ye have not lamented" (Matt. 11:16-17). What does this mean?

One day I was walking along a street in Philadelphia and I heard a little girl of about eight call out to another one to come over and play. Her companion came toward her, calling out, "What are you going to play?" She answered, "Oh, I've got a swell game. Let's play house and you will be father coming home late at night and I'll pitch into you something terrible." Little did she realize the tragedy of the words she was speaking. The other child said, "Oh, I don't want to play that." The one had mourned but the other would not lament. Children play games that include every great emotion of joy and sorrow of human life. Sometimes the other children hang back and do not want to enter into the spirit of the game. But all games are the same to children. A funeral or a wedding; a doctor for high fever or a party for the dolls; all emotions are alike to children.

This is what our Lord meant when He spoke to the people of that generation. "But whereunto shall I liken this generation?" Children playing in the market. Whether it be a game of sorrow or of joy that is proposed, some children hang back. This is the way the people had received the offer of the Kingdom in righteousness. John came as a stern figure of repentance. He was clothed with a garment of camel's hair and his food was locusts and wild honey. His disciples spent many days in fasting. His call was the stern call to repentance. His preaching was the demand for righteousness. The people smiled to themselves and turned away from that picture. Some said that John acted that way because he was possessed of a demon. He had mourned unto them and they had not lamented.

The Lord Jesus came with a personality that was evidently very winsome. He was welcomed among the publicans and harlots. He sat down with sinners to eat and drink, and as a general rule, that class of people desire no spoil-sports about them. We may believe that our Lord was good company, although He never compromised with truth or righteousness. His message interested men. His works amazed them. They followed Him and saw Him heal the sick and give sight to the blind. But He sat with them at their common table, ate their food and drank their wine. His call was the loving call to repentance. His preaching was the invitation to righteousness. There was nothing falsely Puritanical about the Lord Jesus. He was the holy and righteous God of all grace.

Yet they did not accept Him. They said that He was gluttonous and a winebibber. He had piped unto them and they had not danced. So that generation was like a crowd of pouting children who would not play. Neither John's stern call nor the tender grace of the Lord Jesus attracted them. They had evil hearts of unbelief.

And then Jesus looked closer to Himself. He saw the few who were gathered unto Himself. They were able to say, "Behold, we have forsaken all, and followed thee" (Matt. 19:27). So while Jesus saw the whole of the generation under the likeness of the pouting children of the market, He looked down at this first beginning of the new family of the sons of God. "But wisdom is justified of her children" (Matt. 11:19). He was Heaven's wisdom. The book of the Proverbs pictures Him under the figure of Wisdom. The Spirit tells us that Christ Jesus is made unto us, wisdom (see 1 Cor. 1:30). And those who have believed and followed the call to righteousness are wisdom's children. He is justified in putting the Gospel call in the way that He has done. The faith of Noah was sufficient to condemn the rest of the unbelieving world. The faith of the little group who are willing to stake all on the naked Word of God proves to all the universe that the wisdom of God is right. Wisdom is justified of her children.

6

THE FIRST NEW WORD: WOE

To the one who has spent much time with the Word of God, it is not necessary to say that every word in the Scriptures is worth weighing well to find out its meaning. The more we know about the Bible, the more we are sure that God never uses a word for mere literary effect. If there are two words that are almost synonymous, we may be sure that there is a shade of meaning that our Lord wants us to see. The more deeply we study, the more we find that the book yields its rich treasures in ways that would seem small and hidden.

In the passage that we have before us, there are several points that must be noted very closely. We are reading in Matthew 11 and come to the twentieth verse. Those who really wish to know their Bibles should see that we are in new country from this verse forward. Draw a thick black line between the nineteenth and the twentieth verses. There is a great divide here. Truth flows down to opposite oceans from this point. We are face to face with a new aspect of the work of Christ. The Lord Jesus was henceforth a different Man in His action and in His speech. The One Who was the meek and lowly Jesus was about to exhibit His strong wrath in no uncertain way.

The high, resonant tones of the Sermon on the Mount were gone. The stern whip of judgment lashed out. The Lamb displayed, for a moment, His wrath which is to break forth again at His return in glory, and before which all the great of the earth shall cringe and cower. The Lord Jesus was not now offering a Kingdom to the leaders of Israel. He was covering them with stinging rebuke. Instead of miracles of healing, there was the announcement of judgment. The heart of the messages changed from the announcement that the Kingdom of Heaven was at hand, to the pronouncement that hellfire yawned in judgment before the cities which had rejected His righteous offer.

We must state the outline of the truth which we are presenting before bringing out this illustration to its full meaning. We have seen that the key to the life of the Lord Jesus Christ is to be found in that verse which divides His ministry into two distinct parts. We have considered the coming of our Lord to present the Kingdom to the Jews. They rejected His offer because of their stubborn misconception of the prophesied work of Messiah. Their minds were filled with prejudice and they did not have an outlook that would permit them to make any mental readjustment. Sin had blinded their minds beyond any such possibility. They had gazed so long at a blazing light of world glory that they could not bring their eyes to focus on the objects that were placed before them.

In this chapter, we reach the point where Christ is turning away from His people, Israel, and is about to turn to the whole world to present the offer of salvation from sin through faith in His blood. We shall see that there are new words in His vocabulary from this time forth. We shall find seven words, at least, which He speaks for the first time, as recorded here in this central section of Matthew's Gospel. Six of these words were probably spoken on one day—the memorable sabbath chronicled in these chapters. If this truth be established, it becomes evident that the day was the most important in Christ's life up to the day of His death.

The first of these new words is the word of condemnation and judgment upon the cities which were rejecting His teaching. The solemn judgment is rendered, "Woe … woe…" The introduction to this passage indicates the time element in a very definite statement. "Then began he to upbraid the cities wherein most of his mighty works were done, because they repented not" (Matt. 11:20). The Word of God weighs the implications of each individual syllable. Here it is recorded that Jesus began to do something. He began to upbraid the cities wherein most of His mighty works had been done. It was a new tone of voice for the Lord Jesus. If we accept the theory that there was an early cleansing of the temple casting out the money changers, we can understand that such an act could accord with the line of His early work, for the Kingdom which He offered was to be founded on holiness, and certainly, that holiness had to begin in the temple of God.

We must not forget, however, that there are certain great Bible teachers who believe that there was only one cleansing of the temple and that the position of the story in the early part of John's Gospel is not for chronological reasons. But this judgment is quite a different thing. He cried out,

Woe unto thee, Chorazin! woe unto thee, Bethsaida! for if the mighty works, which were done in you, had been done in Tyre and Sidon, they would have repented long ago in sackcloth and ashes. But I say unto you, It shall be more tolerable for Tyre and Sidon at the day of judgment, than for you. And thou, Capernaum, which art exalted unto heaven, shalt be brought down to hell: for if the mighty works, which have been done in thee, had been done in Sodom, it would have remained until this day. But I say unto you, that it shall be more tolerable for the land of Sodom in the day of judgment, than for thee. (Matt. 11:21–24)

This does not sound like the Sermon on the Mount. It has more the ring of the book of Revelation. It is there that we read of the breaking of the seals of judgment and that the Lord Jesus is revealed as the Lamb in His wrath.

> And the heaven departed as a scroll when it is rolled together; and every mountain and island were moved out of their places. And the kings of the earth, and the great men, and the rich men, and the chief captains, and the mighty men, and every bondman, and every free man, hid themselves in the dens and in the rocks of the mountains; And said to the mountains and rocks, Fall on us, and hide us from the face of him that sitteth on the throne, and from the wrath of the Lamb: For the great day of his wrath is come; and who shall be able to stand? (Rev. 6:14-17).

There were certain historical events preceding the Russian Revolution which were like an open window upon all that was to follow in the manifestation of Bolshevism. In 1905, there was a flurry of a revolution which someone has called a dress rehearsal for the vast revolution of 1917. In the passage we are studying in the Scriptures, we have something akin to this when the Lord Jesus broke out in His denunciation of the cities where He had done His work. For it is He Himself Who shall take His place upon the throne of judgment in that day of which He spoke to these cities which had rejected Him.

But it is more terrible here in the Gospel according to Matthew than it is when it is seen in its awful reality in the last book of the Bible. By the time we have reached the end of the New Testament, we are adjusted to the need for uncompromising judgment. The crucifixion scenes have been read. The great passages of the epistles which speak of the great and terrible day of the Lord which is to bring judgment have led us on step by step until we are expecting the righteous wrath of the Lord to break forth.

We are familiar with the strains of the "Hallelujah Chorus." Handel took the words from the apocalyptic scene of judgment. "The kingdoms of this world are become the kingdoms of our Lord, and of his Christ; and he shall reign forever and ever" (Rev. 11:15). All Heaven breaks forth into worship. Hallelujah! But it is a scene of judgment, and our redeemed hearts are glad to join in praise when it occurs. We are convinced that it is fully necessary; we have seen from experience and from revelation that nothing else will do. God must judge this sinful earth and all its iniquity.

But here in the Gospel of Matthew, in the record of the life of the Lord Jesus Christ, these words surprise us like snow in summer. What is this that the Lord Jesus was saying? First, let us remember what He had been saying. He had been telling men that they were to have confidence in God. He had been talking about the lilies of the field and the fowls of the air. He had been telling men that if they were struck on one cheek they should turn the other. He had been going about these villages doing good. In the evening "they brought unto him many that were possessed with devils: and he cast out the spirits with his word, and healed all that were sick" (Matt. 8:16).

And then the scene changes and words that cut and burn come from those lips that had so lately dropped blessing. It is like one of those familiar passages in a symphony, where the composer has soothed the listeners with the soft music of a pastoral scene and suddenly there bursts forth the blare of the trumpets and the roar of the kettle drums announcing the arrival of a sudden storm.

"Woe ... sackcloth and ashes ... day of judgment ... brought down to hell ... more tolerable for Sodom ... " What a change this is! It is the first great announcement that the rejection of the Lord Jesus Christ, the

Son of God, by any individual means rejection of that individual by God the Father. The cross of Jesus Christ is the touchstone of eternity. He had not yet come to the day of His death, but the principles which were leading to His rejection and His crucifixion had already been announced and these cities would have none of them. That is why judgment was pronounced upon them. They were ignorant of the righteousness of God and were confiding only in a false righteousness which had its source in their own efforts. The result was that they would be lost. Later, in the Epistle to the Romans, this verdict is put into words: "…they have a zeal of God, but not according to knowledge. For they being ignorant of God's righteousness, and going about to establish their own righteousness, have not submitted themselves unto the righteousness of God" (Rom. 10:2-3).

Here it is that Christ announced different degrees of punishment. Just as we know that there will be varied degrees of rewards in the future Kingdom, some receiving rewards in addition to their salvation, which is by grace alone, so among the lost there will be a more profound misery, a more terrible punishment for some than for others. Christ made it clear that the condemnation is greater for the cities in which He did His great works, because there had been more light there and the people had not responded to the light. Tyre and Sidon never had seen the miracle-working power of the Lord Jesus Christ. Chorazin, Bethsaida and especially Capernaum had seen the Lord on many occasions. They would be brought down to Hell because they had not repented.

What a word of warning this is for our day! May we not say that if the peoples of Asia and Africa had had the preaching of the Gospel which had been heard in the enlightened lands of America and England, they would long since have come to Christ? We know, of course, that there is no such thing as a "Christian nation." That is a phrase that is used by some who have been misguided as to the real purpose of our God in this age. God is not Christianizing nations; He is saving individuals. Let us therefore give more earnest heed to these things. If you listen to the preaching of the Gospel of Jesus Christ and then refuse to accept Him as your own personal Savior, God says that your condemnation will be far greater than that of those who have never heard the preaching of the Gospel. Many who have heard the Gospel again and again have not yet come to the place of decision. How great is their condemnation! They can never say that they have not had the opportunity of accepting the salvation which God offers to all who will come to the cross and believe His Word about the eternal satisfaction of the blood of Jesus Christ.

At the judgment bar of God those who have rejected the truth that is in Christ Jesus will be forced to recognize that they heard the mighty words of the Gospel, listened to the appeals of those who loved their souls and yet passed these opportunities by, trampling under foot the love of God by their rejection, and that they go to their eternal doom justly. One of the things which will make eternal punishment so terrible will be the fact that all will recognize its entire justice. Those who cry out today against the idea of eternal punishment will be forced to admit as they enter that very punishment that God is just, and that God is holy, and even that God is loving.

It is a most solemn thought. Men will be punished because they have not lived up to the light that they have had. This is a thought that would inspire terror in every honest heart were it not for the words of grace which our Lord then spoke. For any thinking man must admit that he has failed to live up to all the light that he has had. That is why the universal conscience of the race turns to the thought of some religion or other. This is the reason why man has been called a religious animal. To be a member of the human race is to possess a human spirit, and to possess this human spirit is to have the conscience which brings the knowledge of good and evil, with its accompanying recognition that we have not always done that which is good and that we have often done that which is evil.

But there is a way out. There is a way, and only one way, whereby man may lose his load of sin and find rest and joy. There is a way whereby all the righteous demands of God may be satisfied. But there is only one way, and that is God's way. Many years ago, Thomas Binney wrote a great hymn concerning man's approach to God which is sung much too rarely in our churches.

Eternal Light! Eternal Light!
How pure the soul must be
When, placed within Thy searching sight,
It shrinks not, but with undisturbed delight
Can live, and look on Thee.

O how shall I, whose native sphere
Is dark, whose mind is dim,
Before th' ineffable appear
And on my unprotected spirit bear
That untreated beam.

There is a way for man to rise
To that sublime abode
An offering and a sacrifice,
A Holy Spirit's tender energies,
An Advocate with God.

These, these prepare us for the sight
Of holiness above;

The sons of ignorance and night
May ever dwell in th' eternal Light,
Through the eternal Love![1]

It is of that eternal love of which our Lord Jesus spoke in the passage we are studying.

There is a startling contrast once more. For as our Lord had turned suddenly to speak awful words of wrath and condemnation, so He turned back to the very calm of Heaven. There was a moment in which He prayed, and His prayer is recorded. The words are carefully guarded so that we will understand that this is all one sweeping incident, and it is recorded that it was at that time, at that time of judgment, that our Lord lifted up His thought to the Heavenly Father and said, "I thank thee, O Father, Lord of heaven and earth, because thou hast hid these things from the wise and prudent, and hast revealed them unto babes. Even so, Father: for so it seemed good in thy sight" (Matt. 11:25-26).

This is another great statement of principle. The man who trusts in human wisdom and human righteousness is going to reject divine wisdom and divine righteousness. Unless a man is willing to come to that place in his spiritual experience where he will acknowledge that he is incapable of understanding God, of finding God, or of obeying God apart from supernatural help, he will never arrive at that supreme step in spiritual experience which is the miraculous work of God in regeneration within a man's life. Just as people do not send a hurry call for the doctor until they are very conscious of the fact that they are sick, so also do people refuse to acknowledge the necessity of accepting the verdict of God concerning the necessity of the blood of Jesus Christ for the atonement of sin, until they have recognized their own lost

---

[1] "Eternal Light." Words by Thomas Binney, circa 1826. Music Newcastle, Henry Morley, 1875.

conditions. And just as some people, seemingly well, are stricken down by hidden disease which has long been eating at their very vitals, so also there are many who might be called by the world "wise and prudent," refuse the simple wisdom of Christ and the prudence of salvation through the righteousness of the Savior.

But the man who is willing to be as a child, as a babe, in the presence of the all-wise Creator and Savior, will find that the choicest secrets of Heaven and eternity are revealed unto him. Not only is he the object of this confidence on the part of God, but he is also the object of a miraculous work of creation within his own being. Thus, he is born again, with a life and a righteousness which are not his own by right, but which become his through faith in Jesus Christ.

And then the passage concludes with a breath-taking invitation. I veritably believe that this was one of the most important moments in the history of the human race. This is the first time that a true Gospel invitation was ever given to this world. It is the second new word. The Lord Jesus Christ had turned away from the narrow insularity of a national work because He had been rejected by the people to whom He came. But at that moment He opened His arms wide to the whole of the race and said, "Come unto me, all ye that labour and are heavy laden, and I will give you rest. Take my yoke upon you, and learn of me; for I am meek and lowly in heart: and ye shall find rest unto your souls. For my yoke is easy, and my burden is light" (Matt. 11:28–30).

Here we see the reverse of the medal. Not only does the refusal of light condemn men to the greatest degree of punishment, but the acceptance of the gift of God brings the rest and joy for which the heart of man yearns.

This invitation was a new step in the ministry of the Lord Jesus. He had come unto His own, the Jews, with the offer of the earthly Kingdom, and His own received Him not.

But now He turns. Now He pronounces woe upon the cities. Now He spreads forth His hands to all who labor and are heavy laden. What a new thought this is! To those who labor with the thought of obtaining salvation and who are heavy laden with the sense of their failures, Christ offers rest. In every religion in the world except in the revelation of God in Christ, men are toiling, toiling to become acceptable to God. In every instance there is complete failure, for God must demand absolute perfection and can never accept less than that from the effort of man.

Just here, then, the wisdom and power of God is manifested. Christ said, "Come unto me,… and I will give you rest." In these simple words we have the revelation of the claims of Christ, the revelation of the love of Christ and the revelation of the power of Christ.

7

THE SECOND NEW WORD: COME

Suppose that a man should walk into the room where you are now seated, and should say to you, "I am God Almighty. Just do what I tell you to do and I will settle all your problems." You certainly would have every right to be very suspicious of such a character. Your mind would immediately come to one of two conclusions. You would think that the one who made you such an offer was either a subject for an asylum or a penitentiary. In all probability the man would be the victim of some terrible delusion, and if his demented condition were a potential danger to the public, he would be put away where his folly could not harm.

There have been men, however, who have made astounding claims concerning themselves when they were in their right mind. In these days, as in all times, there are slippery gentlemen who will make a racket out of anything, so long as they can find gullible victims who are willing to part with good money to pay them for their deception. To call a man crooked or crazy is indeed a harsh verdict, yet there are times when society is forced to render such a judgment. Is there any other word we could apply to the statements of one who would thus claim to be God? Nevertheless, we stand face to face with a Man Who makes just such a claim, but our findings are quite different in this instance, for it is the claim of the Lord Jesus Christ.

He came to the hearts of men with just such a claim. The first time in the Gospels that the Lord Jesus made a plea for faith and trust, we find these words on His lips, "Come unto me, all ye that labour and are heavy laden, and I will give you rest. Take my yoke upon you, and learn of me; for I am meek and lowly in heart: and ye shall find rest unto your souls. For my yoke is easy, and my burden is light" (Matt. 11:28–30).

This is the very first Gospel invitation given by our Lord Jesus. It is the full realization of the significant time of this invitation that gives full point to its conclusiveness. Rejected by His own, He opened His arms wide to the weary universe and offered men that which can never be found outside His gift. He told men that He would solve all their problems. Salvation from sin, peace in the midst of trouble, and contentment in the midst of need—all these things were promised to weary hearts by this Man, Christ Jesus.

"Come unto me,… and I will give you rest." How important this word is to help establish, once and for all, Christ's own estimate of Himself. Did He grope around to find Himself spiritually, as some would have us believe? What nonsense such a thought is to those who really know the Bible and the claims of Christ! In every part of His ministry, we find the unhesitating assurance of the eternal Son of God, manifested to destroy the sins of the world.

On the day that He stood for the first time in the synagogue of Nazareth and read the Old Testament prophecies of Isaiah, He claimed that He was the object of those prophecies. "The Spirit of the Lord is upon me, because he hath anointed me to preach the gospel to the poor; he hath sent me to heal the brokenhearted, to preach deliverance to the captives, and recovering of sight to the blind, to set at liberty them that are bruised, To preach the acceptable year of the Lord" (Luke 4:18-19). These are the words spoken by Isaiah the prophet and recorded in the sixty–first chapter of his prophecy. But these are the words which the Lord Jesus took as the text of His first formal utterance, as we read in the fourth chapter of Luke. And when He had read them to the congregation, He took the seat of the teacher and said, as the eyes of all that were in the synagogue were fastened upon Him, "This day is this scripture fulfilled in your ears" (Luke 4:21).

His message never changed. From the first moment when He claimed to be the object of the Messianic prophecies, on throughout His whole life, the heart of His claims was never altered. "I and my Father are one" (John 10:30). "[H]e that hath seen me hath seen the Father" (John. 14:9). "Before Abraham was, I AM" (John 8:58). The leaders of Israel took up stones to stone Him, because that He, being a man, as they thought, yet made Himself equal with God. He did not seek to correct their opinion. He did everything to strengthen and support that idea. He said that His words were more lasting than heaven and earth (see Matt. 24:35). Those who built upon His words were building upon the solid rock, but those who did not build upon them were building upon the sand (see Matt. 7:24-27). In the very first Gospel invitation, the Lord made a statement that is so simple and yet so stupendous that it dwarfs all comparison.

If a man came to you today and told you that you could find rest and joy and peace by following him, you would be sure of one of two conclusions. Such a man would be trying to fleece you out of your funds in order to line his own purse, or else his poor reason has tottered from the throne and he is a wandering simpleton; nonetheless crazy, though he may be harmless.

But common sense refuses these two conclusions as regards the Lord Jesus Christ. There is no one in the world who would brand

Him as a hypocrite. The universal testimony of all generations, both of His friends and of His enemies, is that He was essentially a good man. Pilate found no fault in Him. The centurion declared that this was indeed the Son of God. The thief on the cross confessed that this Man, Christ Jesus, died unjustly. He was the Just and the Innocent. He was called the Holy One.

Are we then to conclude, since He was certainly not a conscious fraud, that He was an unconscious fraud? Was His a disordered intellect? We are quite aware of the fact that a book was recently published in France which has attempted to support this fantastic theory. But the critics, Jew and Gentile alike, were unanimous in proclaiming the folly of the attempt. Thus, if both horns of the dilemma are impossible, there is no conclusion but the supernatural one: this Man was none other than God Almighty, and He had the right to offer rest to the human heart because He alone was capable of giving that rest for which the soul longs.

But not only is this great invitation a revelation of the claim of the Lord Jesus Christ as to His own personality and being, it is also a revelation of His love. He saw the need of the world and knew that there was only one possible remedy for its need. It is that which He offered to supply. The Lord Jesus Christ is eternal. He saw clearly not only the narrow picture of the generation of His contemporaries within the limited confines of the small land where He was born, but down through the ages, and throughout all the lands of earth. That is the reason why He told men that He would give them peace if they would come unto Him.

Later on, when He was about to go to the cross to die, He cried out to the men of His day, "O Jerusalem, Jerusalem, thou that killest the prophets, and stonest them which are sent unto thee, how often would I have gathered thy children together, even as a hen gathereth her chickens under her wings, and ye would not!" (Matt. 23:37). Ye would not. That was the tragic word in His day, and that is the tragic word today. Jesus Christ had all power and all wisdom. He knew what men needed most. He knows what men need most today. But the difficulty is that they will not believe Him. "And ye will not come to me, that ye might have life" (John 5:40), were the words that He spoke to those who were in such great need. It was this knowledge of the world's need and what would satisfy that need which limited the program of Jesus Christ and caused Him to offer just what He did present to men.

There is a man who is a reporter for one of our daily newspapers. One evening, we met at a meeting where a new cult was being presented. All evening the emphasis had been placed by the speakers on a form of religion that mentioned the name of Jesus but had nothing to say about salvation through faith in His atoning death. Any polite Gandhi could have said as much as these speakers said. On the way out, we asked the reporter what he thought of the meeting. "Not much," he replied, and then continued, "I can see how you would disagree with what was said, but my disagreement is on entirely different grounds. I disagree with them for the same reason I disagree with you." We asked him how he disagreed with us, though we knew that he made no pretence of being a Christian in the Bible sense of the word. He complained that there was no social emphasis in our beliefs. This is, of course, absurd in the light of all the social works that have followed in the train of evangelical Christianity. There can be no doubt of the fact that the history of most of our great educational institutions, medical schools and hospitals, orphan asylums, homes for the aged and the feeble minded will show that evangelical believers in the Lord Jesus Christ were instrumental in establishing them.

Undoubtedly, however, this gentleman meant that there was no socialistic emphasis on the part of evangelical believers. While the greatest social works of our civilization have been byproducts of true Christianity, there are some phases of life that many Christians have never been willing to touch, simply because they know that there must be a change in human nature before these things can be accomplished. Christ lived all His life in a land where the tramp of Roman legions echoed along the roads, yet He never lifted up His voice against war. Indeed, He said that there would be wars and rumors of war to the very end of the age. He knew that the collective heart of man was but the total of the individual hearts. He had said, through the prophet Jeremiah, that this heart was deceitful above all things and desperately wicked (see Jer. 17:9). He lived all His life among social conditions where half the population was in slavery to the other half, yet He never lifted up His voice against slavery.

Rather, He said that the servant was not greater than the master, and through His disciples, taught that a man was to remain in that social class where he was when salvation found him. It is only individual faith in the work of the Lord Jesus Christ that can reach into the heart of the greatest of the social ills. Where the needs are merely physical, Christianity and its imitators can indeed provide asylums, food, clothing, doctors and nurses. But the collective influence of all the Christians in the world is not sufficient to change even one sinful, greedy heart. The reason why Christ never spoke against war or slavery is because, like any good physician, He worked against causes rather than against mere symptoms. It needs more than influence, individual or collective, to change men. It needs the supernatural work of regeneration. "Ye must be born again."

His heart must have burned against the visible iniquities of His day, while the emphasis of His message was "Come unto me,… and I will give you rest." In the day in which we live, the followers of the Lord Jesus have the same choices to make, and the same message to declare.

For a minister of the Gospel of Jesus Christ to spend his time talking about international peace and conciliation is to give his voice to sound and fury. Yet no one hates war more than the Christian who longs for the day when the Lord Jesus shall come and put an end to such horrors. We have looked upon hundreds and hundreds of faces of men that have become monstrosities through the barbarism of modern methods of warfare. That is enough to give an undying hatred of war. But our knowledge of truth and the realities of life is such that we know that war will continue so long as men have sinful, selfish hearts. There are probably thousands of men within the confines of all the great cities of the world who would gladly welcome the return of war tomorrow, providing that they could have war-time prosperity in their business once more. So instead of preaching against war, we say to individual hearts, "Come unto Christ, and He will give you true peace."

There are other miseries of our day that call for the fiercest wrath of the true believer, but this wrath is curbed by the certain knowledge that earth has no palliatives for its bitterest woes and deepest afflictions. The other day I walked down a street at the moment when some poor, unfortunate people were being ejected from a house. Their few cheap bits of household goods were being piled upon the sidewalk and a curious crowd of onlookers was watching the procedure. Immediately, I thought of those Bible characters, James and John, the two disciples whom Jesus called the "sons of thunder." I remembered that on a certain occasion, they came to Him, saying, "Lord, wilt thou that we command fire to come down from heaven, and consume them…?" (Luke 9:54), referring to some people who had been uncharitable. For a moment, there flashed through my mind that it would be a great gesture to gather together some of the unemployed and force the authorities to return the miserable furniture to the shelter of the house. This furniture was but kindling wood to those men who were dragging it out to the street, but it was blood and tears to the people who had added penny to penny in the days when love was young and life was gay. I thought, for a moment, that if we could break up such hellish practices in desperate times like these, at least the newspapers could not say that the leaders in the breakup of the eviction were radicals and Bolsheviks.

But after that first hot wave of flaming resentment against the system that makes such conditions possible, I realized that my business was not to work on symptoms but upon causes, and that the only way to reach the heart of men's need is to point them to Christ Who promised to give them comfort in the midst of sorrow and rest in the midst of turmoil. So we continue to preach the cross, which is foolishness to them that perish, but unto us who are saved, it is the power of God.

Therefore we conclude that Christ's great Gospel invitation was a revelation of His love, since He knew that He alone could calm the raging sea within the hearts of men and reach beyond the surface of their need into the very center of their souls. "Come unto me, all ye that labour and are heavy laden, and I will give you rest." He sees you, He knows you, and He invites you to come to Him.

This great Gospel invitation is also a revelation of the power of our Lord Jesus Christ. For this invitation to come unto Himself, is not to be classified in the field of theory and speculation, but rather as a most practical way, the only way, indeed, to get out of theory and speculation and into contact with the real power of God. Christianity is worthless if it is not able to bring to the heart of the individual the reality of forgiveness from sin and the power of the risen life of Christ to dwell within our lives.

A few years ago the age–old controversy between believers and infidels became front page news in the daily papers. This was because it was news for the public to discover that the Voltaires, the Tom Paines, and the Ingersolls of our day were not outside the Church, attacking as enemies, but that they were ordained to the ministry and were attacking from the pulpits. Theological phrases were to be found in headlines, and the man in the street saw as much about the Virgin Birth of Christ in his daily paper as he has seen about economics during later years. While that phase of the struggle was being waged, there appeared a little four-line poem that recalls this first great invitation.

> Though scholars disagree,
> I find it daily true,
> Christ Jesus does for me
> What only God can do.[1]

That is, of course, an unanswerable argument. God alone can forgive sins. This was admitted by the Pharisees of Christ's day when He spoke forgiveness to the paralytic lying before Him. So Christ accepted their statement, but proved that He was correct in saying "Man, thy sins are forgiven thee," by adding to His words of grace a deed of power. For He concluded, when the Pharisees reasoned that His statement was blasphemy, "What reason ye in your hearts? Whether is easier, to say, Thy sins be forgiven thee; or to say, Rise up and walk? But that ye may know that the Son of man hath power upon earth to forgive sins, (he said unto the sick of the palsy,) I say unto thee, Arise, and take up thy couch, and go into thine house" (Luke 5:22-24). Christ Jesus did for this man what only God can do. And the miracle which Jesus Christ works within the hearts of those who trust Him is even greater than that which He wrought upon the withered limbs of the lame of His day.

There are thousands of us who can testify that Christ Jesus does for us what only God can do. And if we are asked for proof, we are able to say,

---

[1] Source unknown.

> I heard the voice of Jesus say,
> "Come unto me and rest;
> Lay down, thou weary one, lay down
> Thy head upon my breast!"
> I came to Jesus as I was,
> Weary, and worn, and sad;
> I found in him a resting place,
> And he hath made me glad.[2]

This is proof, laboratory proof. This is something that must be accounted for by the skeptic. No amount of psychological reasoning can do away with it. The great experience of the man who has really met Christ as Savior and Lord cannot be classified under what students would call "The Varieties of Religious Experience." There may, indeed, be ten thousand kinds of counterfeits, but there is only one reality. Those who have thus met with the Lord and Savior have a vocabulary of experience that is impossible to anyone else.

Imagine a Buddhist, a Mohammedan, or the follower of any other human being in this world being able to say that which we can so truly say about Christ. No other name could be fitted into this verse:

> I came to Jesus, and I drank
> Of that life-giving stream;
> My thirst was quenched, my soul revived,
> And now I live in him.[3]

---

[2] "I Heard the Voice of Jesus Say." Words by Horatius Bonar in *Hymns Original and Selected*, 1846. Music by John B. Dykes, 1868.

[3] Ibid.

This is indeed a power that is infinite. To still the storm in the human heart is God's greatest work. Over in the Psalms there is a verse which says, of God, that He "stilleth the noise of the seas," and that is great; "the noise of their waves," and that is even greater; but the passage concludes that He stilleth "the tumult of the people," and that is greatest of all (Ps. 65:7).

He can quiet the storm in your heart if you will come unto Him. He can take away the burden of your heart if you will come unto Him. He will stop the gnawing of your conscience if you will come unto Him. He will answer every doubt of your heart and mind if you will come unto Him. He will fully satisfy your every longing if you will come unto Him. He will soothe your pain, lift your care, comfort you in sorrow, and heal your broken heart, if you will come unto Him. It is He Who can dry your tears if you will come to Him.

This is His only condition: come to Him. What He offers you is a gift. Be not slow to take it. This gift includes pardon from sin, peace in the heart, purity in the soul, power in the life, hope for the future, for it is the gift of Himself. He is our peace. Come unto Him. He will give you Himself.

8
CHRIST AND THE SABBATH

It is, perhaps, not at all strange that the great struggle between the Lord Jesus Christ and the leaders of Israel began over a simple question of form and ceremony. The wars of religion in all ages have been fought over secondary and inconsequential things. But at times, in back of the trivial there is the eternal. The Church of the East split from the Church of Rome ostensibly because there was a theological disagreement concerning the brief Latin expression *filioque* in one of the creeds. In back of that there was the earthly desire for power and self-aggrandizement on the part of two opposing groups of men, neither of which would acknowledge the leadership of the other. Many of the so-called religious wars have been fought upon mere pretence to hide the desire of some king, baron or prelate for fat fields or wealthy cities.

But beneath the difficulty between the Pharisees and the Lord Jesus Christ there lay eternal principles which would permit no compromise whatsoever on the part of our Lord. The leaders of the ecclesiasticism of that day were entrenched behind their forms and ceremonies. Their hearts were godless and their lives were full of hidden sin that was nonetheless terrible because it was not primarily moral sin. We must never forget that spiritual sin is always condemned by God with a condemnation that is undoubtedly greater than for any other form of sin.

In the twelfth chapter of the Gospel according to Matthew is recorded the definite climax and crisis of the conflict between the religionists and the eternal Son of God. The leaders had no heart for the Lord Jesus Christ because they had no heart for the things of God. They were the successors of the long line of stiff-necked persecutors who had stoned the prophets and killed those who had been sent unto them. Now Christ presents Himself as the Lord of the sabbath. The open break with Israel is about to take place.

It is to be noticed that the first words of this chapter are "At that time." This clause definitely links these events with those that have just been enacted. Christ came unto His own and His own received Him not. But He read their unbelieving hearts and began to pronounce a message of judgment upon the cities because they had rejected Him and His works. He had come and taken up His abode among the poor. He fellowshipped with the publicans and the harlots; "the best people" were outraged. This Man Who lived down in the slums! What did He think He could do with the people who were self-respecting? Did He not know that those people with whom He associated simply did not belong? These were the thoughts that filled their proud hearts. They had long since selected a vocabulary with which they damned all the loose living poor and those whose money had some common taint. "This fellow eateth with sinners," they complained, and in their hearts they called Him a glutton and a winebibber.

It has always been the same way. The man who steals a million or so from the "reorganization" of some public utilities corporation will still be welcomed among these charming hypocrites, but the man who has reached out his hand for bread for his children is considered to be a vulgar criminal. The Lord Jesus Christ received the stigma of His associates, and pronounced His curse upon the cities as a result. With this curse there was the free offer of salvation for all who labored and were heavy laden. He offered rest of heart freely to all who would come.

It was at that time that the rift became an open break. The story is very clearly told in the simple words of Scripture: "At that time Jesus went on the sabbath day through the corn; and his disciples were hungred, and began to pluck the ears of corn, and to eat. But when the Pharisees saw it, they said unto him, Behold, thy disciples do that which is not lawful to do upon the sabbath day" (Matt. 12:1-2). Here was an act, and a criticism of that act. The Lord then proceeded to answer the charge that His disciples had broken the sabbath.

Let us realize, first of all, that the sabbath was and is particularly a Jewish institution. It is the seventh day, and not the first day. It was on the seventh day that God rested after the six days of creation. This was not the sabbath. There was no sabbath until the time of the giving of the Ten Commandments from Mount Sinai. God tells us very definitely that it was at that time He "madest known unto them thy holy sabbath" (Neh. 9:14). It was a sign upon the Jews. The only thing to which it can be compared is the rite of circumcision. Sabbath keeping was a spiritual sign upon Israel as circumcision was a physical sign upon them. It distinguished them from all other peoples. When the law was fulfilled and the age of grace came into being, sabbath keeping came to an end. What we observe in this dispensation is not the sabbath at all, but the day of the resurrection of the Lord Jesus Christ. It is an entirely different thing.

When anyone calls Sunday the sabbath he is making a mistake as wrong as if he should call Easter Day "Christmas" or Thanksgiving Day "the Fourth of July." It would be impossible in many of the great languages of the earth, such as Italian and Spanish, because the seventh day, Saturday, in those languages is named the sabbath (*sabato* and *sabado*, respectively). There is no reference in any language for hundreds of years after Christ in which Sunday is called "the sabbath." And the greatest authority on the use of words in the English language, the vast work edited by Gilbert Murray, *A New English Dictionary on Historical Principles*, says,

> The notion that the Lord's day is a "Christian Sabbath," or, more commonly, a substitute for the (Jewish) Sabbath, occurs in theological writing from the fourth century onwards, but was not popularly current before the Reformation. In English, Sabbath as a synonym for "Sunday" did not become common till the seventeenth century.

Any attempt to foster this double error, linguistic and theological, is a direct outgrowth of the same spirit that the Pharisees showed when they attempted to condemn the followers of the Lord Jesus for transgressing their traditions.

Let us guard this statement with one observation, however. We are not taking away from the first day of the week, the Lord's Day, Sunday, any of its sacredness. The child of God, born again through faith in the redemptive work of the Savior, is not going to turn Christian liberty into license. We hold the first day of the week sacred, but that holding is for Christians only. On that day we delight to remember that we worship the living Lord Jesus Christ Whose resurrection is the guarantee of our salvation and the guarantee of our future resurrection and life eternal. This is enough to cause us to be busy telling others about Him on that day and on every day, and in gathering together on the first day of the week as is definitely ordained in the Scriptures. But let us come in the spirit of Christian liberty. Any other spirit is a dead sabbatarianism which is contrary to the Gospel.

The following differences have been pointed out between the sabbath of the Jews and the first day, the resurrection day, of the Christian. Israel was commanded to observe the seventh day; the Church is privileged to enjoy the first day. The keeping of the seventh day was the test of Israel's moral condition; the observance of the first day is a proof of the fact that the Church has been accepted by God through the risen Lord Jesus Christ. The sabbath manifested what Israel could do for God; the first day of the week declares what God has done for us. Ours is a glorious liberty, but we must not forget the solemn call of the Spirit through the Apostle, "For, brethren, ye have been called unto liberty; only use not liberty for an occasion to the flesh, but by love serve one another" (Gal. 5:13).

These leaders of Israel were mistaken, therefore, when they told the Lord that His disciples were doing that which was not lawful for them to do on the sabbath. For there was not a word in the law of God that even hinted that men could not eat when they were hungry. The Jews were very proud of their sabbath keeping and had added much to the Word of God. All that God had said is recorded in the midst of the Ten Commandments:

> Remember the sabbath day, to keep it holy. Six days shalt thou labour, and do all thy work: But the seventh day is the sabbath of the Lord thy God: in it thou shalt not do any work, thou, nor thy son, nor thy daughter, thy manservant, nor thy maidservant, nor thy cattle, nor thy stranger that is within thy gates: For in six days the LORD made heaven and earth, the sea, and all that in them is, and rested the seventh day: wherefore the LORD blessed the sabbath day, and hallowed it (Ex. 20:8-11).

Here is the expression of a brief and concise principle. But the men of those days tried to interpret it in their own way. They had hearts that were not at rest in the Lord and His righteousness, so they imagined all sorts of foolish rules that they laid upon the people.

If we read the *Mishna* of the rabbis we shall be amazed at the extent of their folly. According to these traditions, a tailor might not go out with his needle nor a scribe with his pen. Clothes might not be examined by lamplight. Wool might not be dyed during the week if the natural processes would not be accomplished by the sabbath. Clothes were not to be dried by the hot air of a stove. A wound could not be wiped. A chair or seat could not be dragged as this might involve producing a rut, and this would be digging. Women were not allowed to look in a mirror lest they see a white hair and be tempted to pull it out, thus supposedly breaking the sabbath. The rabbis had listed thirty–nine forbidden tasks which they called parent or father—labors and scores of others which were "descendant" labors because they grew out of the former. Rabbis differed with each other as to whether, after a bath on the sabbath, the whole body should be dried at once, or limb after limb. They were practically united, however, that a man could not spit on the ground on the sabbath, as that might make a furrow, but that there was no such difficulty in spitting upon a stone and that such an act would not involve a breach of the sabbath. If a man bathed in mineral waters he might not carry his towel home as he might be carrying some mineral particles with it. And so on, *ad nauseam*.

Let it not be forgotten that it was this type of mind with which the Lord Jesus had to do when He was here on earth. How did Christ silence His accusers? In the same way in which He had met Satan at the temptation. When Satan tempted Him, He answered, "It is written … It is written …" It was with the Word of God that He showed them the folly of their tradition.

A fine ship may be covered with barnacles, but navigators are not directed in their course by the barnacles. God had given the law; the rabbis had covered it over with the barnacles of their tradition. Christ scraped them off. He pointed to an incident in the life of King David, when the latter was rejected and a fugitive. Here was the King of Israel, forced to take refuge from those who sought his life, forced to find his food in the land where he was ruler. He walked into the temple and took for himself and his men the shewbread which, according to the law, was for the priests alone.

Christ reminded these Pharisees of that incident. "Have ye not read," He asked them, "what David did, when he was an hungred, and they that were with him; How he entered into the house of God, and did eat the shewbread, which was not lawful for him to eat, neither for them which were with him, but only for the priests?" (Matt. 12:3-4). The real sting in this answer lies in a verse which Christ did not quote, but which they who heard Him must have known well. For in the passage of the Old Testament where the story is told, David answered the priest of the temple and said, "…the bread is in a manner common, yea, though it were sanctified this day in the vessel" (1 Sam. 21:5). Do you not see what this means? David was the Lord's anointed king. He was rejected, and while he was rejected there was nothing in all Israel that was holy. So he took the bread because, in that moment, he was greater than the bread.

The Lord Jesus then pointed out the fact that the priests in the temple offered sacrifices on the sabbath day. This would be considered as labor, yet it was not breaking the law. Why not? Because the sacrifices were sacrifices of grace. By means of this act, God's sovereign love saved men, pardoning their sins when they did not deserve it, simply because He had chosen that method of setting aside sin, foreshadowing that He had planned for the Messiah, the Lord Jesus, to do when He came as the Lamb of God, taking away the sin of the world. When grace is at work, it is higher than the law.

Then came the climax of His statements, "But I say unto you, That in this place is one greater than the temple" (Matt. 12:6). This was a claim that they could not misunderstand. The temple was the place where the Lord Jehovah of Hosts was worshipped by His people. For Jesus

Christ to stand up and say that He was greater than the temple can mean but one thing. Only the Being Who is worshipped is greater than the house of worship. This is another of the many declarations in which He claimed to be God Almighty. He continued His statement by saying that they, the Pharisees, would not have condemned the guiltless if they had understood the words of the prophet Hosea, "I will have mercy, and not sacrifice" (Matt. 12:7; see Hos. 6:6). It was redemption grace that God wanted, and not merely the blood poured out upon the altar.

There are many in our day who cry out against the idea of blood sacrifice. They see in it that element of horror which any right-minded person could not fail to comprehend if they stood and saw the flashing knife, the surge of warm blood and the struggles of the dying victim. Yes, there is nothing beautiful about it. It is positively ugly. God recognizes that fact, but He is saying that sin is still more ugly and that the only way to be rid of sin is by the mercy that God provides at the sacrifice. Every time a lamb was slain upon the temple altar, God was looking at the death of His only begotten Son on the cross.

So Christ came to His conclusion. We might paraphrase it as follows: "You have accused My disciples of breaking the law. But all they have done is to transgress your foolish rules which were written down, no doubt, with the thought of helping men to try to keep the original law, but which became in the hearts of this wicked people the end and not the means. I am not looking into the hearts of men to try to find slavish keeping of a set of rules, I am looking for men who know and realize the loving heart of a tender Father. He set aside the law that He had made Himself concerning the temple bread when His chosen King David was a fugitive. So you cannot expect God to look with favor upon any act whatsoever which proceeds from hearts that have no love toward the Father, and which reject His Son." No sabbath keeping could be acceptable to God from hearts that were rejecting Jesus Christ.

Finally, in one majestic phrase, He sets them right forever. "For the Son of man is Lord even of the sabbath day" (Matt. 12:8). He Who had spoken from Mount Sinai to Moses in the giving of the law stood before them to tell them that He was greater than the law He had made. He was the promised Messiah, come to bring righteousness. They wanted no righteousness. They wanted mere legalism. The hollow shell meant very much more to them than the kernel, the crust much more than the bread.

The Lord Jesus left these men and walked into the synagogue. There was a man who had a withered hand. The Pharisees with angry hearts had followed Him. They hated Him—O! how they hated Him— but they did not yet dare give vent to their hatred. He had silenced them with His knowledge of the Word of God. They had no answer to this Man Who claimed to be the Lord Jehovah and Who demonstrated His omniscience in such a way. There was no answer to what He said. Though they hated Him, they followed Him. They wanted to find something in Him upon which they could base their accusations. They had tried to dismiss Him from their minds by calling Him a glutton and a winebibber because He had associated with the poor and despised. Now, they seek to dismiss Him from their minds by calling Him a lawbreaker. As time went on they would think up still more terrible charges against Him. They would accuse Him of blasphemy. They would even say that He was the prince of demons, working by the power of Satan. But on this fresh sabbath morning they had not yet allowed their hatred to become articulate.

The world today is very conscious of Christ. Someone has called this a Christ-haunted age. The magazines of the world carry a constant stream of articles about Him and His principles. Seldom do we find a word that is truly Christian, but there are millions of words written about so-called Christian things. We do not recall having seen more than half a dozen articles in secular magazines in the last ten years which have been truly Christian. Men follow Christ at a distance and talk about Him and His Word, trying to find an answer for Him that will satisfy the unrest in their hearts. But they will not come to Him to receive the gift of life.

The Pharisees followed Christ that morning to watch His dealings with the sick. They asked, "Is it lawful to heal on the sabbath days?"— and the God Who alone knows the motives of men's hearts adds the awful sentence—"that they might accuse him" (Matt. 12:10). It is interesting to notice that this question shows that they believed in His power to heal. They had undoubtedly questioned many a man or woman who had been healed, and knew from personal experience many people whose tortured bodies and souls had been healed by this wonderful Man.

If we had the privilege of being transported back through time in order to stand and watch the eyes of the Lord Jesus on any given occasion, we would choose for that occasion one of the moments when He looked upon some sinner with compassion. But could we choose two moments to catch His look, this would, perhaps, be the second one. Only the redeemed could bear to see this look. You may be sure that the Pharisees shifted their gaze or looked down to the ground.

"What man shall there be among you," He asked, "that shall have one sheep, and if it fall into a pit on the sabbath day, will he not lay hold on it, and lift it out?" They all knew that they had done just such things. Then He added, "How much then is a man better than a sheep?" (vv. 11-12). There are men in our godless society today who do not think that men are better than sheep. In the days of our Lord there were men who besought Him to leave them because they loved swine better than the soul and body of a poor tormented man. In our day there are leaders who are putting the welfare of banks and corporations above the welfare of human souls. We believe, before God, in the light of eternity and in the knowledge of the Bible that these men who exploit human beings for gain will suffer in the lowest of hells forever. Be not deceived; God is not mocked.

The Lord stood before these hypocrites and said to the poor withered man, "Stretch forth thine hand." And we read that "he stretched it forth; and it was restored whole, like as the other" (Matt. 12:13). Christ's message was that of the supreme worth of the individual. In a recent number of *Forum*, a leading liberal claims that there is no social order which can be established in which the individual would be given the supreme worth. It is bad enough under capitalism, he says; it is even worse under communism. This latter may be true, but when this Man Christ Jesus comes again He will establish a millennium upon this earth, a long sabbath over which He will be Lord, and a man will be considered as worth more than a sheep.

But the only hope of the individual while we wait for that day to dawn is that we shall enter into the consciousness of forgiven sin through faith in His blood. He stands before you today, wherever you may be reading these words. He says to you, "Stretch forth thy hand." There are many of us who have obeyed this call and have found that as we stretched forth the hand that was bound by sin it reached even unto the cross of Calvary and there we found life eternal, and joy that this world cannot know. Beware lest you take your place with the Pharisees!

9
THE THIRD NEW WORD: GENTILES

There are certain personalities that grow tense under heavy strain. In the measure that difficulties grow, irritability increases. There are other natures that act in quite another way. In the measure that difficulties grow, their calm and strength become greater.

Submarine navigators tell us that no storms reach very deep into the ocean. There is calm weather a hundred feet down, no matter what the height of the breakers that roar on the surface. It was thus in the life of our Lord Jesus Christ. His most bitter enemies raged. He was calm. In the moment of great climax when His rejection first became manifested publicly, we have one of the mightiest pictures of the Lord. He was not merely strong like an oak that does not bend before the wind, even though the branches and leaves betray the passing presence of the storm, but like the unruffled depths of the sea, or like the unswerving motion of the North Star.

The hatred in the hearts of the religious leaders had come to the point where they had held a council against Him, how that they might destroy Him (see Matt. 12:14). It was then that there occurred an act so dramatic and so significant that we must not fail to see it. We read that "when Jesus knew it"—knew that they were holding a council against Him—"he withdrew himself from thence" (v. 15). It was a sad day for

Israel. When the Messiah of Israel withdrew Himself from His people, there could be nothing but bitterness left in their cup.

We know, of course, that the responsibility for the death of Jesus Christ does not rest upon the Jew alone. Humanly speaking, the guilt is divided between Jew and Gentile, and among men of every kindred and generation. We must admit our part of the responsibility. He was dying there for our sins. But from the point of view of God, He was giving His life. When the leaders thought to destroy Him, they were imagining a vain thing. Christ said, "I lay down my life, that I might take it again. No man taketh it from me, but I lay it down of myself. I have power to lay it down, and I have power to take it again" (John 10:17-18).

One commentator has said that Christ withdrew at that moment in order to protect Himself from the danger of the Pharisees. Rather, the withdrawal of Christ from the plotting leaders was an ordered gesture of the Son of God, significant, as was everything He did. From that day to this, the Jews have been set aside. Not cast off, but set aside. Christ had withdrawn from them. From God's point of view, their clock was stopped. Soon, we believe, it will start ticking again, when the Lord Jesus returns. Remember the prophecy of Hosea, "After two days will he revive us: in the third day he will raise us up, and we shall live in his sight" (Hos. 6:2). "But, beloved, be not ignorant of this one thing, that one day is with the Lord as a thousand years, and a thousand years as one day" (2 Pet. 3:8). The "two days" of Israel have almost run their course. Soon will the glorious third day dawn for the chosen people.

As the Lord Jesus withdrew from these evil, unbelieving hearts, there were other multitudes which followed Him, and He healed them all. He told them not to make Him known. He knew that the hour of His death was not yet come, and He did not want to stir up the jealousy of these envious Pharisees until the time was ripe. Then, He would go forward to meet the enemies who would move upon Him with sword and stave, and would submit to their will.

But first, He was going to reveal the tenderness of His heart. Filled with compassion for the needs of these people, He would pour out His life in a passion of devotion to these poor misguided ones. They were the fickle crowds. They did not have the genius of command. Too long had they followed their leaders like dumb, driven cattle. It was for these crowds that Jesus wept. It was to these crowds that Jesus ministered. "And the common people heard him gladly" (Mark 12:37). The leaders did not know the plan of God: "…none of the princes of this world knew: for had they known it, they would not have crucified the Lord of glory" (1 Cor. 2:8).

The Lord Jesus Christ loves the masses of the people today. As in the day when the earth was waste and desolate and the Spirit of God brooded over the face of the deep, so today, while the leaders of the world have reduced the hundreds of millions to misery and need, the Lord Jesus yearns over them and longs to draw them to Himself. This is man's day, in which the Lord is permitting men to do as they please. Satan is the prince of this world, the god of this age. But there is to be a great overturning, greater than the French Revolution, greater than the Soviet Revolution, for it is to be accomplished by the power of the Lord Jesus, Who will brook no interference in that day. Then "the last shall be first, and the first last" (Matt. 20:16). So, His heart yearns toward the multitudes today, and He calls you to Himself.

In withdrawing Himself from the leaders of Israel, He was drawing Himself to another group. It is startling to find the third new word "Gentile," on the lips of the Jewish Messiah, but here it is, "That it might be fulfilled which was spoken by Esaias the prophet, saying, Behold my servant, whom I have chosen; my beloved, in whom my soul is well pleased: I will put my spirit upon him, and he shall shew judgment to the Gentiles" (Matt. 12:17-18; see Isa. 42:1-4).

A short time before, when the twelve disciples had been instructed and sent forth on their first preaching mission, the Lord had told them definitely that they were not to go to the Gentiles (see Matt. 10:5). From this moment there was the complete reversal of this former plan. Now He announced that He Himself was to fulfill the promises that had long since been made of the Messiah; He would show judgment to the Gentiles. What a mighty change had come into His ministry! It is the understanding of this phenomenon that will open up the Scriptures and give a more complete comprehension of the purpose and the method of the life of the Lord Jesus Christ.

In our day it is difficult for us to understand the effect of such an utterance upon the minds of those who heard Christ speak. We are Gentiles, and we are accustomed to the message of the Gospel that we have had for many generations. But He was speaking to people who had been brought up to look down upon the Gentiles. We have only to look at two or three other passages of Scripture to see into the minds of the people of that day concerning the Gentiles. St. Paul, writing to the Ephesian church, which was composed of Gentiles, reminds them of their background. We read there, "Wherefore remember, that ye being in time past Gentiles in the flesh, who are called Uncircumcision by that which is called the Circumcision in the flesh made by hands; That at that time ye were without Christ, being aliens from the commonwealth of Israel, and strangers from the covenants of promise, having no hope, and without God in the world" (Eph. 2:11-12). This is what the Apostle Paul was able to say to the Gentiles more than thirty years after Christ spoke the words we are studying. The verdict, given by God Himself, is that at that time the Gentiles were God-less, hopeless and Christ-less. When he was accosted by a heckler, former British Prime Minister Benjamin Disraeli was correct in answering, "Yes, I am a Jew; and when your ancestors were eating acorns in the heart of the German forest, my ancestors were giving law and religion to the whole world."

One more biblical proof of the strangeness of this word on the lips of Jesus may be found in the action of the Jews toward Paul when he used it in Jerusalem. Paul went to Jerusalem late in his life, and his friends succeeded in getting him to compromise his spiritual position in order to try and win over the bitter enemies. The plan was for him to go into the Jewish temple and mingle with those who were performing the religious rites of the temple worship. He was to take a vow upon himself in accordance with the custom of the Jews. But his presence was soon discovered and a great uproar ensued. Finally, the Roman soldiers came and surrounded Paul, leading him off to prison. He spoke with the leader of the troops and asked permission to address the crowd. When permission was granted he began to speak in Hebrew, at which there was a great silence.

His speech is recorded in the book of the Acts of the Apostles. The men who had desired his life a few moments before were now perfectly calm as Paul recounted the story of his early life and of his conversion. The crowd did not even make a motion of impatience when he mentioned the name of Jesus of Nazareth, or when he spoke of the resurrection of Christ and of His supernatural position as Lord. But when he said that he had had a vision from God Who had spoken to him saying, "Depart: for I will send thee far hence unto the Gentiles" (Acts 22:21), there was an immediate change. A wave of fury burst over the audience at the mere mention of the word "Gentiles." The passage says, "And they gave him audience unto this word, and then lifted up their voices, and said, Away with such a fellow from the earth: for it is not fit that he should live. And as they cried out, and cast off their clothes, and threw dust into the air…" (Acts 22:22-23). It was the word "Gentiles" that precipitated the riot.

And in the passage that we are studying, we find it on the lips of the Lord Jesus Christ. He was quoting the forty-second chapter of Isaiah, one of the great passages that spoke of the Messiah Who was to come. Those who heard Him in that day realized that He was indeed quoting out of the Hebrew Scriptures, and there was no answer that can be made to the claim that Isaiah prophesied that the Messiah should have a phase of His work among the Gentiles. Note well the new words in our Lord's vocabulary. Judgment upon the cities, a free offer of salvation to all who would come and receive the gift, and now the promise extended to the Gentiles.

At this point in Matthew's record we catch a glimpse of the heart of the Lord as He was pleased to reveal Himself through the prophetic Word that He now claimed for Himself. Once more we must point out that the Lord Jesus Christ definitely claimed to be the object and fulfillment of the Old Testament prophecies. There are those who pretend that Christ never claimed any supernatural position. How such an assertion can be substantiated in the light of the evidence is beyond comprehension. At every point in His ministry there is the clear picture of His own thought about Himself.

Here in the moment of His rejection He quoted the prophet Isaiah. What should the Messiah do when He is rejected of His people? Shall He exercise His judicial prerogatives and blast them with the fire of His wrath? No. The day of His patience is about to run. Man shall have his day. God will put all organization and government into the hands of man and will allow him to run it as he pleases, and when the final chaos has been reached, He will gather out the faithful witnesses which He has had in every generation, and will then pour out the cup of His wrath upon the world. But in that moment when the Pharisees held council against Him, He took to Himself the Word of Jehovah concerning the Messiah and announced that He would then show mercy to the Gentiles.

But how? Let us read the verse. "He shall not strive, nor cry; neither shall any man hear his voice in the streets. A bruised reed shall he not break, and smoking flax shall he not quench, till he send forth judgment unto victory. And in his name shall the Gentiles trust" (Matt. 12:19-21). This is a claim to tenderness. Let us not forget that tenderness is a strong virtue. There is nothing weak or feeble, nothing wavering in true tenderness. In fact, we might define tenderness as being the action of strong love.

He did not need to strive. Had He desired, He could have spoken the word that would have spelled their doom. But the moment of doom was still future. We must not forget, however, that He possessed that latent power. In the garden of Gethsemane, when the soldiers came to arrest Him, He came forth saying, "Whom seek ye? They answered him, Jesus of Nazareth. Jesus saith unto them, I am he" (John 18:4-5). The form of the answer was probably such that it included the name of Jehovah, which no Jew would speak. The great "I AM" was speaking. The eternal Creator held out His hand to be taken. We read that when He spoke this answer, "they went backward, and fell to the ground" (John 18:6). He could have spoken at any moment and judgment would have flashed forth from His person, banishing the rebels from His holy presence forever.

But He was waiting for the slow unfolding plan of God. Therefore He worked in God's way. He did not strive nor cry. His voice was not heard in the streets. Man cannot do anything without struggle and noise. This Man would not work in man's way, but rather in God's way.

And then the verse goes on with that wonderful illustration of the tenderness of Christ: "A bruised reed shall he not break, and smoking flax shall he not quench." Every member of the human race has a trait of destruction within him. A boy walks down the street and sees some ants on the sidewalk. He will stop for two or three minutes while he crushes them all, running after each one in order to put his foot down in death. And then the boy walks on. He jumps into the air to catch the branch of a tree. He breaks off the branch and tears the leaves from the stem. With the switch that is left he slashes at the blossoms of the flowers which hang over the wall and causes the buds to droop and die. He reaches for a stone and flings it in the general direction of a bird or a cat. He plucks the rose and tears its petals apart and scatters them as he goes. All this may be in the course of a ten-minute errand. And it is a reflection of a trait characteristic of human nature.

But the Lord Jesus Christ did not have this trait in His being. His was the strong tenderness of the Creator God. He did not lift up His hand to hurt in nature, so we know that we may approach Him in the most implicit confidence. The slightest roughness would quench the smoking flax, but the Lord Jesus will blow the feeblest light to flame.

There may be someone who reads these words who is afraid to come to Christ. Fear not. He will receive you. A bruised reed shall He not break. The shepherds who watched their flocks in the fields often passed their time making a sort of flute, the pipes of Pan, from the reeds that grew wild. They played their plaintive melodies upon these reeds, but soon the reeds became bruised. They were then worthless, and with a careless gesture, the shepherd would break the reed and throw it aside. There was no good in it. There was nothing to do, but get another.

But the Lord Jesus said of Himself that He would not break the bruised reed. You may be aware of the fact that the melody has gone out of your life. There was a time when life was young and gay. Sin had not yet bruised you. You were happy, and walked with a spring in your step. But now you have a bit of cynicism in your smile, at those times when you find it possible to put forth a smile. You have lost your illusions. You have become tarnished. Whatever may be your trouble, whether you have been downed by sin or by circumstances, you feel that you are near the end of your self and you are wondering whether or not there is anything worthwhile. Listen once more to the Lord Jesus Christ. A bruised reed shall He not break. He will not cast you aside. And moreover, your reed, that is worthless to the world, He can recreate under the magic of His touch and bring into your life melodies more wonderful than any of the songs you sang in those days before despair came.

> Down in the human heart, crushed by the tempter,
> Feelings lie buried that grace can restore;
> Touched by a loving heart, wakened by kindness,
> Chords that were broken will vibrate once more.[1]

That is the truth of God. Broken chords and bruised reeds give forth harmonious sounds once more, for He takes us up out of the horrible pit, out of the miry clay, sets our feet upon a rock, establishes our goings, and puts a new song in our mouths (see Ps. 40:2-3). Thank God, our Lord Jesus Christ, the God of music, is our Savior. The Author of all harmony will not despise the bruised reed.

It would be pleasant to be able to end the chapter here. It would be so agreeable to close on a note that might promise melody and tenderness to all. But that is not possible because of the wicked heart of unbelief that possesses so many. The society in which we live is organized for grief, while bitterness is its fruit. Selfishness and greed fatten on human distress, and exploitation is the very blood stream of the life of the world. The reeling world cries out, "How long O Lord? How long?" and God gives us back the answer from Heaven.

For at the same moment that our Lord took the measure of the Pharisees and withdrew from them, He also announced that the days

---

[1] "Rescue the Perishing." Words by Fanny Crosby. Music by W. Howard Doane, 1869.

of His humility would not last forever. The evil heart of man will take advantage of the one who does not strive or cry, and whose voice is not heard. The world has learned to call the tempered steel of the sword of the Lord "softness," simply because He does not flash its cutting blade as the world would do in His place. But listen to these words that at the same time strike terror and bring joy. "A bruised reed shall he not break, and smoking flax shall he not quench, till…" Ah! So there is to be an end of His patience! He shall not act in full strength "till he send forth judgment unto victory." Listen to those two words: judgment, victory. They sound out like the ringing of a death knell, or they peal forth with the joy of the wedding. It all depends where you stand in relation to this Man, the Christ of God. You must have Him in one of these two ways—judgment or victory. We thank God that we know forever just what our situation is with reference to this Man. He has taken our judgment. That is past forever. There is nothing left for us but His victory. You can know this too.

He shall send forth judgment unto victory. It is coming. Righteousness shall reign upon the earth. Man sends forth justice but she goes lame before reaching her goal. Man sends forth justice, but she is given a sack of gold so heavy that the burden tires her and she stops to rest on the way. Man sends forth justice but she is flattered by the wayside and turns to smile on the one who spoke. But when our Lord Jesus Christ sends forth judgment it shall be unto victory. Which will you have? The judgment or the victory? The Bible is very definite in its prophecies concerning the future. There is a picture of this sending forth of judgment. We read these words, "And the kings of the earth, and the great men, and the rich men, and the chief captains, and the mighty men, and every bondman, and every free man, hid themselves in the dens and in the rocks of the mountains; And said to the mountains and rocks, Fall on us, and hide us from the face of him that sitteth on the throne, and from the wrath of the Lamb: For the great day of his wrath is come; and who shall be able to stand?" (Rev. 6:15–17).

The only ones that shall be able to stand are those who shall be standing in Him.

> On Christ, the solid rock, I stand;
> All other ground is sinking sand.[2]

---

[2] "My Hope Is Built on Nothing Less." Words by Edward Mote, 1834. Music by William B. Bradbury, 1863.

10
DEVIL OR GOD?

There are more than four hundred thousand words in the New International Dictionary. In addition to these, there are many more thousands of derivatives. Numerous fascinating stories are connected with words and their origins, and many enlightening shades of meaning to be gathered from the comparison and contrast of words and the ideas they express. There is an interesting paragraph in Crabb's *Synonyms*, where the author draws a sharp distinction between the words "comparison" and "contrast." We are all familiar with these words and know the difference between them. We understand that those things which are alike may be compared, while only opposites may be contrasted. A comparison is made between two shades of red, but a contrast is made between black and white.

Crabb says of these two words, "Comparison is of a practical utility, it serves to ascertain the true relation of objects; contrast is of utility among poets; it serves to heighten the effect of opposite qualities…" Now if contrast is useful to poets, then God is a wonderful poet. Certainly He has given us many marvelous comparisons and many amazing contrasts.

God is a poet, not only in the marvels of nature, but He is also the Author of true art in words, since He has given us the Bible with heavenly truth in perfect form, and since He is also the Creator of the minds of Homer, Virgil, Dante, Shakespeare and the host of others. Of literature, as well as of Ceylon it may be said that every prospect pleases and only man is vile. We must never forget that pure truth and beauty of form and expression are all the gift of God.

In the twenty-second to thirty-second verses of Matthew twelve, we are faced with one of the greatest contrasts in the Bible. God Almighty arrays Heaven and Hell in one scene and lets us look at the two. He demonstrates that His ways are not our ways and that His thoughts are not our thoughts. We see that His ways and thoughts are, indeed, above ours, as the heavens are high above the earth.

But in considering this scene of contrast, we must have our hearts fixed upon the great need of men, the searching judgments of God, and the clear call of Christ to individual hearts. It is well to delight in the artistry of the scene and in the drama of the Word, but the sole need is that which will touch our souls. If our hearts glow and our minds thrill as we take in the heightened figure of our Lord Jesus Christ as He contrasts Himself with His enemies, it is also true that our hearts are sad and our minds perplexed as we see the hatred that can be brought against this Man, Christ Jesus. It is against the background of the tenderness of Christ that this scene is laid: "He shall not strive, nor cry; … A bruised reed shall he not break, … till he send forth judgment unto victory" (Matt. 12:19-20).

Swiftly the scene changed to one that pictures judgment. This scene took place undoubtedly on that memorable sabbath upon which His disciples had been accused of lawbreaking because they gathered wheat to appease their hunger. Christ had revealed the motives of the leaders of the people by healing a poor cripple. The envy and jealousy of the Pharisees knew no bounds. They plotted to destroy Him. He had come unto His own and His own received Him not.

It was still on this memorable day of rejection and turning that the next step toward the climax occurred. The crowd was following Jesus. Someone brought in a poor man, blind and dumb, possessed of a demon. Jesus healed the man so that he saw and spoke. The crowd realized that they were in the presence of no ordinary man and cried out, "Is not this the son of David?" (v. 23). There was no mistaking the implication of this cry. The Son of David was none other than the Messiah Who was to come. To call Christ the Son of David was to acknowledge His deity and His messiahship.

But the leaders of the Jews who were hovering nearby were filled with rage and greater envy as they heard this cry of the people. They were afraid to voice all that they felt, but their thoughts were filled with hate. They were thinking that Jesus had His great power through the prince of the demons.

It is worthy of note that these enemies of the Gospel admitted the truth of the power of Christ. These men would have exposed any trickery had there been any. The Lord Jesus was surrounded by fierce and bitter enemies, who had most hostile eyes. Mark tells us that these men were a deputation sent down from Jerusalem. They were the keenest scouts of the Pharisees, and were the choice of the lot for cunning, yet they were forced to admit that Jesus Christ was working miracles. They tried to explain it, but in giving their explanation they admitted the truth of the fact. Nicodemus had come to Christ before this with the same admission but with an entirely different explanation. He had said, "Rabbi, we know that thou art a teacher come from God: for no man can do these miracles that thou doest, except God be with him" (John 3:2). In all these explanations, the important fact is that these men admitted the supernatural powers of the Lord Jesus Christ. They could not explain Him on natural grounds. The keenest minds of His day, sharp and critical, were forced to admit that He was outside the common run of men.

The explanation of the Pharisees was that the power of Jesus Christ was Satanic power. What He had done they could not deny, so they said that it was done by the power of the prince of the demons. This explanation is as foolish as those that leave out the supernatural. We would be amazed at the stubborn willfulness of unbelief had we not been warned by our Lord of the deep-seated reasons for this denial— reasons which lie buried in the recesses of the sinful human heart. Every once in a while, we meet just such arguments in our dealings with men today. With an airy gesture of contempt, they would dismiss the whole question and say with a firm tone that it cannot be so simply because such things are not so.

A good many years ago, commenting upon this habit of some unbelievers, a Scotsman said,

> It is very easy to solve an insoluble problem if you begin by taking all the insoluble elements out of it. And that is how a great deal of modern thinking does with Christianity. Knock out all the miracles; pooh–pooh all Christ's claims; say nothing about Incarnation; declare Resurrection to be entirely unhistorical, and you will not have much difficulty in accounting for the rest; and it will not be worth the accounting for...

Indeed, men have refined the processes of explanation during the course of the centuries that have followed one another since this day when the Pharisees attempted to account for Christ in this way; but though the explanations have changed, the process remains the same, deep down underneath. It is the attempt of unbelief to account for the living Lord Jesus Christ. Over against all such suave explanations there will ever stand the Lord's plain declaration, "And this is the condemnation, that light is come into the world, and men loved darkness rather than light, because their deeds were evil" (John 3:19).

We have never found an honest sceptic. Some men claim to be honest sceptics, but before probing very deep the truth comes out. If a man is an honest sceptic he will soon cease to be a sceptic. A man might claim to be a sceptic about the multiplication table, but if he were an honest sceptic, he would soon learn that six times seven are always forty-two and that eight times seven are always fifty-six, and his honesty would lead him to certain definite fixed conclusions, and he would find himself no longer a sceptic. With the dishonest sceptic, it is quite another matter. If you ask him to count out the eight times seven to see for himself, he will add a piece from his pocket or do away with a piece to make the answer come out according to his preconceived bias.

The honest man must admit that Christ stands out above the whole race and that every succeeding generation has been passionately addicted to the problem of explaining Him. Someone has said,

Where did this Man, so fair, so radiant, so human and yet so superhuman, so universal and yet so individual, where did He come from? and where did the Gospel, which flows from Him, and which has done such things in the world as it has done—where did it come from? "Do men gather grapes of thorns, or figs of thistles?" If it is true that Jesus Christ is either mistakenly represented in the Gospels, or that He made enthusiastic claims which cannot be verified; and if it is true that the faith in a resurrection on which Christianity is suspended, and which has produced such fruits as we know have been produced, is a delusion; then all I can say is that the noblest lives that ever were lived in the world have found their impulse in a falsehood or a dream and that the richest clusters that have ever yielded wine for the cup have grown upon a thorn. If like produces like, you cannot account for Christ and Christianity by anything short of the belief in His divine mission. Serpents' eggs do not hatch out into doves. This Man, when

He claimed to be God's Son and the world's Savior, was no brain-sick enthusiast; and the results show that the Gospel that His followers proclaim rests upon no lie.

Not only was their explanation totally inadequate, it was positively foolish. These men admitted the miracle but said that the power of Christ over Satan came from Satan. Christ answered the claim with a simple argument that stands alone as pure logic. He said, "Every kingdom divided against itself is brought to desolation; and every city or house divided against itself shall not stand: And if Satan cast out Satan, he is divided against himself; how shall then his kingdom stand?" (Matt. 12:25-26). This answer of the Lord, as it stands, is sufficient to demonstrate the folly of the accusation brought against Him. He was not working with the devil against the devil, which is another way of expressing the thought of the Pharisees. Such an idea is clearly preposterous. This would be civil war within the forces of the prince of the power of the air. That idea is not sufficient to explain the mighty person and work of the Lord Jesus Christ.

What then is the true explanation of His power and being? He announced the truth in completing His refutation of their folly. He said, "But if I cast out devils by the Spirit of God, then the kingdom of God is come unto you" (v. 28). The most splendid king who ever sat upon the throne of France, Louis XIV, was the author of the famous statement, *L'état c'est moi*—"I am the State." This Man, Christ Jesus, was making a claim far more wonderful. Indeed, a human sovereign may so control the powers of the state that he may claim to be the state, the very personification of the state. But the Lord Jesus, God's King, was claiming to be the Kingdom of God. "For in him dwelleth all the fulness of the Godhead bodily" (Col. 2:9). This was the explanation of His power. Where He acted, it was God acting. When He spoke, it was God speaking.

If Christians understood this claim, there would be many things simplified in the teaching of the Bible. For example, there are those who claim that the Kingdom of God is within the hearts of all men. There are some very broad, liberal interpretations of the Scripture which seize upon the famous phrase, "the kingdom of God is within you" (Luke 17:21). They would try to make it mean that the Kingdom and power of God are to be found within the hearts of men, and that all that is necessary is to appeal to this highest element within man. Such an idea is palpably nonsensical. In the first place, Jesus said these words to a group of His bitterest enemies, the very men who later crucified Him. The true translation is, "the kingdom of God is in the midst of you," or "among you." It is the same idea that He gave when they accused Him of working through the power of the devil. "No," was His answer. "The work I am doing is the proof that I am the Messiah. Heaven's King is in the midst of you. This is the power which you see at work."

He then announced that He was at war with Satan, but that He was perfectly able to overcome that sinister power. He had effectively bound "the strong man," Satan, and thus He was able to release the poor demon-possessed man from the clutch of the devil. What a word of joy this is to every sin-bound soul! You who know what it is to feel the claims of sin, there is salvation for you! Christ Jesus the Lord has come to earth. He went to the cross and died, so that through death He might destroy him that had the power of death, that is, the devil (see Heb. 2:14). This was why He took a human body: that He might be nailed to the cross, that at Calvary, by the wisdom and power of God, there should be the eternal answer to the problem of your sin, and that Satan might be forever deprived of his power over those who come to God in Christ. There are many of us who can testify to the personal experience of this victory that is ours in Christ. We know that our Lord has bound the strong man and thus has been able to come into our lives and do His victorious work.

The conclusion of this incident is amazing. Christ knew that His person and work had produced a crisis that would admit no compromise. There might be some place for argument in a comparison of scarlet and vermilion, but there can be no hesitation when it is a contrast between black and white. This is the Lord's stern declaration. "He that is not with me is against me; and he that gathereth not with me scattereth abroad" (Matt. 12:30). This is a call of war. In times of peace, governments can afford to be benevolent and to allow the expression of soap-box opinions that are subservient to national unity. But when war has been declared there is only one thing to do. Every nerve of the nation must be steeled to the tasks of war.

This is also true in the spiritual realm. The Lord Jesus Christ had come unto His own and His own received Him not. He had come as Heaven's King and they had called Him an emissary from Hell. They took council against Him how they might destroy Him. The issue was joined. They had declared war. Their action had been the opening of hostilities. Christ took up the gage of battle. Men must make their choice. It is devil or God. They had stated the case. There is no middle ground. It is impossible to be neutral in such a conflict. If any man tries to be neutral, he becomes a foe.

On the road to Jericho a man lay wounded and bleeding. A priest passed by, and seeing the man lying near death, turned not a hand to aid him. The Levite passed by on the other side: These men were not with the dying man; therefore, they were against him. So far as they were concerned, he was condemned to death. The Samaritan was with him to help him; therefore, he was for him.

This homely truth of the story of the Good Samaritan is ten thousand times more applicable to Christ Himself. He stood before the world accused of working with the power of the devil. It is impossible for the human mind to conceive the affront that this accusation made upon His holiness. It is no wonder that Christ said that anyone thus speaking against the Holy Spirit of God Who was within Him, doing the works through the yielded human nature of our Lord, had committed a sin that could not be forgiven. Here was more than sin. Here was open alliance with the powers of Satan. Here was the enmity of the seed of Satan against the Seed of the woman. Here was cold-hearted malice in the fury of desperation.

Christ did not call these men to decision. They were past feeling. They were joined to their idols and were to be let alone. His words were overheard by the crowd, however. This is why He spoke as He did. He turned upon these leaders in a moment with words more acid than any ever spoken by any other man. The fourth new word is "generation of vipers." Would the bystanders hear and heed Him? The choice was now urgent. On the surface it was Jesus or the Pharisees. Down underneath it was, in reality, the choice between God and the devil. This is why the Lord Jesus Christ said, "He that is not with me is against me; and he that gathereth not with me scattereth abroad." It must be one or the other. "Mr. Facing–both–ways" is always standing around when the leaders are cutting the division sharply. The Lord loves the man who has not made his decision and speaks in terms that will reach through to the man's will.

As the LORD says, "…turn ye, turn ye from your evil ways; for why will ye die…?" (Ez. 33:11). This is God's Word to you today. The time is short. We are not looking for the passing of the years that lead to death. We are looking for the sudden, glorious return of the Lord Jesus Christ. But when He returns He shall not come as the meek and gentle Jesus Who would not quench the smoking flax nor break the bruised reed. Then He shall come to send forth judgment unto victory.

Paul writes to the Corinthians, "…now is the accepted time; behold, now is the day of salvation" (2 Cor. 6:2). Do not think that because you know the plan of salvation in your mind that you can put off letting it come down into the heart. One of the saddest conditions of which we have ever heard is that of a man in an asylum who continually recites Bible verses. These words of life echo back and forth in the porches of his ears, but the promises no longer reach into the center of the will. We must not forget that it is in one of the latest of the epistles that the Holy Spirit speaks of those who are "past feeling." They have rejected God for so long that He has rejected them. It is a terrible thing to be given up by God. If there is the slightest concern within your being over your spiritual state, you can know that you are not beyond the reach of salvation. If a man is really concerned because of his lost estate there can be but one reason for that concern: it is because the Holy Spirit is still speaking to him, convincing him of sin. Therefore, leave the folly of your rejection. You may be born again in this very moment if you will accept God's Word about your own lost condition and His Word about the value of the work which Christ accomplished upon the cross for you.

"He that is not with me is against me; and he that gathereth not with me scattereth abroad." Who is this Man, Christ Jesus? Devil or God? There is no other possible verdict. The issue is clear-cut. You must take your position with Him or you remain in your sin, dead, and under the necessary wrath of God.

You MUST decide for Christ. If procrastination were merely the thief of time it would not make so much difference. But procrastination is the thief of eternity.

11
JESUS ANSWERS BACK

Here are some words that men consider "fighting words." Even the most peaceful and calm temperaments, among non–Christians, are stirred to wrath upon being called certain names. Yet we feel safe to say, no man in this world ever called another man by epithets so severe and burning as did the Lord Jesus Christ.

At first glance, this is rather surprising in the One Who is so often known as the meek and lowly Jesus. It is true that He said of Himself, "I am meek and lowly in heart," but He was speaking of His attitude toward those sinners who approached Him with the thought of repentance in their hearts. When the emissaries of the scribes and Pharisees sought Him out in order to try to trap Him, He not only let them know that He had read their hearts and knew their plans and their motives, but He spoke to them in terms so plain that judgment was flashing from His person. They fell back from before Him in wonder and dismay.

Think for a moment of the phrases that this Man Jesus Christ used in speaking to those who had declared themselves as His enemies. He never used these terms behind the backs of those whom He was describing. When He had some terrible verdict to render, it was given directly to those who were involved. This made it all the more severe. He added new meaning to the term of hypocrite. But this was merely a beginning. "Whited sepulchers"—"dirty cups"—"generation of vipers." The Lord Jesus took words that bring up revolting scenes to the mind and applied them to these false leaders.

Suppose you picked up a cup that appeared to be clean but when you brought it to your lips you discovered that there was filth in the liquid. There would be a gesture of disgust as you put it hastily away from you. This is the picture He would give us of these religious leaders. Filth cloaked by cleanliness, is the description of their hearts. Suppose yourself to be walking in an old churchyard reading inscriptions on ancient stones. Suddenly you find the soil giving way beneath your feet and you slip up to your knees in an old grave. There is a feeling of horror as you hasten to extricate yourself from the contact with dead men's bones. This is the picture that Christ gives us of these religious leaders. Corruption clothed with dignity is the description of their hearts. Suppose you are working in a rock garden on a fine spring day. You turn over a stone and discover a den of poisonous snakes under your hand. You draw back with that quick, cold feeling of repugnance and loathing fear. This is the picture that Christ gives us of these religious leaders. Slimy death, cloaked with respectability, is the description of their hearts.

The important aspect of this truth, from the point of view of our line of argument, is that Jesus Christ spoke first against these men on the day of the crisis in His ministry. It was spoken on the day when He turned from His own, the Jews, in order to go His way to the cross that He might offer the Gospel freely to all who would come unto God by Him. He pronounced judgment upon the cities where His work had been rejected, announced that the Gospel was now open to all who labor and are heavy laden, and withdrew Himself from the leaders of Israel, saying that He would now show mercy to the Gentiles. It was then that the leaders of the people sneered at Him, saying that His power came from the devil.

This was the background against which the most terrible verdict ever yet heard by man was delivered from the lips of the Son of God; He said that they had committed the unpardonable sin. They had gone so far in the stubbornness of their rejection that they had attributed the work of the Holy Spirit to the devil. There could be no forgiveness for this sin. This was because a mind which had reached the stage of rejection that would behold the Lord Jesus Christ as He went about doing good and would see nothing but the work of Satan in that manifestation of divine power, was so manifestly a mind yielded to the power of Satan that there would be no possibility of bringing repentance. Their sin was indeed unpardonable because of the condition of their hearts.

The true explanation of the unpardonable sin must be stated, in passing, for the benefit of those who have been concerned at some time or another with the fear that they had been guilty of a sin that is unpardonable. Certainly we are not permitted to deny all the doctrines of salvation and keeping by grace in order to explain this passage. The unpardonable sin, therefore, can never be committed by anyone who has been born again. And, so far as an unsaved person is affected, it is evident that the unpardonable sin could not have been committed by anyone who is troubled about any kind of sin. For conviction and concern about sin is a work that is done in the heart by the Holy Spirit. It must necessarily follow, therefore, that a heart where the Spirit is yet working cannot be a heart which has been abandoned by the Spirit of God.

So the judge of all hearts pronounces His verdict. "Either make the tree good, and his fruit good; or else make the tree corrupt, and his fruit corrupt: for the tree is known by his fruit. O generation of vipers, how can ye, being evil, speak good things? for out of the abundance of the heart the mouth speaketh. A good man out of the good treasure of the heart bringeth forth good things: and an evil man out of the evil treasure bringeth forth evil things" (Matt. 12:33-35).

This passage is often quoted, and often misquoted. When Christ cried out, "Either make the tree good, and his fruit good; or else make the tree corrupt, and his fruit corrupt," He was telling these men that there had to be a radical change in their lives. They had not been born again. They possessed only an old nature but they were seeking to adorn it with a substitute righteousness. Men can be deceived by this outward appearance, but God looketh upon the heart and is not satisfied with its condition. Men must have a miraculous work performed within their lives so that there will be a tree of life within on which good fruit may grow, or they must recognize that the fruit which God demands cannot grow upon the old dead wood of the human life apart from Christ.

Why will men persist in taking such a passage as this and using it to contradict all the rest of the teaching of the Bible? It is precisely like the great passage in which Jesus said, "They that be whole need not a physician, but they that are sick. But go ye and learn what that meaneth … for I am not come to call the righteous, but sinners to repentance" (Matt. 9:12-13). Did Christ mean that the righteous did not need saving and so announce that He had not come to call the righteous? Of course not! Such a thought is to contradict all that God teaches about the sinful heart of man. The truth is that Jesus Christ was telling men that there is no such thing as a righteous man so far as God is concerned. "I am not come to call the righteous, but sinners to repentance," means that if a man will persist in thinking that the kind of righteousness which he can produce could ever satisfy God, that man is in such a perverted state of mind that there is no salvation for him. But if, on the other hand, he will come to the place where he admits before God that he is a lost soul, deserving the condemnation of the just wrath of God, then he has put himself in that place where the grace of God can flow upon him, full and free, and provide him with a righteousness which is none other than the righteousness of God in Christ.

It is precisely the same thought that is in view here. These Pharisees were dead wood masquerading as living trees, just as though a man should tie green branches to a dead stump. God can never be satisfied with such a masquerade. Christ is asking that the mask be removed. Either come to the place where the miracle of regeneration is wrought within so that there will be good tree and good fruit or else stand openly as the children of Satan, enemies of God and capable of bringing forth only evil fruit.

The idea that it is possible to judge whether or not a man is a Christian by the outward manifestations of his life is an idea that Jesus rejected on several occasions. The disciples asked if they were to root up the tares that the enemy had planted in the midst of the wheat. The Lord told them that they were to let them alone, for in seeking to destroy tares they might root up some of the wheat. God has His program of good works which He desires the believer to experience. He tells us that the born again ones have been "created in Christ Jesus unto good works, which God hath before ordained that we should walk in them" (Eph. 2:10), but He also tells us that some Christians are "babes in Christ," and are "carnal," walking as unsaved men so that it would be difficult for the outsider to tell the difference (see 1 Cor. 3:1-3).

On the other hand, it is easy to see that there are some who are not Christians who are able to counterfeit the Christian graces. You must not think that a person is saved because he has a sweet life. Every once in a while you will meet someone who will tell you that Dr. So–and–so must be a fine Christian because he has such a sweet, gentle manner. We have heard thus described some of the most errant Christ rejectors of our day. There is a difference between a man's fruit and a man's life and character. Every man's life is what God says it is, and he is subject to all the temptations of the race, possessing an old nature which can do nothing to satisfy God. But a believer possesses also a new nature which is the very life of Christ dwelling within. In the measure that a life is yielded to His presence, Christ will live His life within.

So when Christ described the working of the false teachers, He was not talking about their characters so much as about the results of their teaching and their policies. "Beware of false prophets," He said, "which come to you in sheep's clothing, but inwardly they are ravening wolves. Ye shall know them by their fruits. Do men gather grapes of thorns, or figs of thistles? Even so every good tree bringeth forth good fruit; but a corrupt tree bringeth forth evil fruit. A good tree cannot bring forth evil fruit, neither can a corrupt tree bring forth good fruit. Every tree that bringeth not forth good fruit is hewn down, and cast into the fire. Wherefore by their fruits ye shall know them" (Matt. 7:15-20).

Suppose we were to attempt to judge the Lord according to those standards that are accepted in many quarters today. We can well imagine a scene in a Palestinian home during the time Christ was here on earth. Someone would say, "Well this Jesus cannot be a good man, for what He is saying does not make for peace. Now the Pharisees are men of peace. They are such good men. I have seen them praying in the market place. They give tithes of all they possess. They want harmony. But this Jesus is a controversialist. He uses such terrible language. He calls these men 'generations of vipers,' and 'hypocrites.' Surely we must see that by their fruits ye shall know them, and we shall have to choose the Pharisees."

And in the days of St. Paul, how easy it would have been to make a case against him! He even called men by name in accusing them of false doctrine. Euodia and Syntyche were to stop fighting (see Phil. 4:2). Hymenaeus and Alexander were to be delivered unto Satan that they might learn not to blaspheme (see 1 Tim. 1:20). Hymenaeus and Philetus were teaching that the resurrection was past (see 2 Tim. 2:17). Demas had forsaken him (see 2 Tim. 4:10), and Alexander the coppersmith had done him much evil (see 2 Tim. 4:14). John wrote that Diotrephes loved the preeminence (see 3 John 9).

What false doctrine it would be to interpret "by their fruits ye shall know them " in such a way as to condemn these Spirit-filled men! Were Paul and John not to be held in honor because they had thus acted? What folly it would be to say that the Pharisees, soft-voiced and smiling, were to be revered above the Christ Who turned over the tables and drove out the money-changers! No! Ten thousand times No! When our Lord said that "by their fruits ye shall know them," He was not talking about the outward appearance of their lives, but about the spiritual fruit that resulted from their work.

We see this today as well. Parents send young people away from a small-town home into a college where they will come under the teaching of cultured, refined agnostics. The young people go back home with an arrogant attitude toward their parents, saying that modern science has done away with the Bible and that the parents' faith is a "hang over" from a departed era. A prominent man recently said that he was not sending his second child to college because he had had such a heart-breaking experience with the first. These are the fruits of the refined and peaceful agnostics. But those who are good trees, by the supernatural life of the Lord growing within, will bring life in the midst of the desert as they go forward with their work and witness.

We must never forget that God told us that when we are looking for the devil we must not forget to look, among other places, in the pulpit. In writing of the "false apostles" and "deceitful workers," the Holy Spirit said, through Paul, that these were "transforming themselves into the apostles of Christ. And no marvel; for Satan himself is transformed into an angel of light. Therefore it is no great thing if his ministers also be transformed as the ministers of righteousness" (2 Cor. 11:13-15). These ministers of righteousness may have beautiful characters, but their doctrines sweep like a blow-torch across the lives of men, scorching and withering all with whom they come in contact.

Men must be born again. God cannot be satisfied with the saccharine substitute of the self-righteous. The character efforts of the human heart can take men to Hell but never to Heaven. Men must be born again. The tree must be made good and the fruit good, or the day will come when men will be forced to come out from under their false thinking and accept themselves for what God knows them to be: children of the devil. For this seems to be the inner meaning of the name that Jesus Christ called these men. They were a "generation of vipers." Way back in the book of Genesis, where we read of the first appearance of Satan as a malignant enemy, we find him called a serpent. In the last book of the Bible God speaks of him as "that old serpent, which is the Devil, and Satan" (Rev. 20:2).

These Pharisees were the brood of that father. In the moment in which God pronounced the curse upon Satan, He said, "And I will put enmity between thee and the woman, and between thy seed and her seed; it shall bruise thy head, and thou shalt bruise his heel" (Gen. 3:15). It is universally recognized by Bible students that this is probably the first promise of the Messiah, the Lord Jesus Christ, since He is so thoroughly identified as the victim of the malice of Satan. Later, in the New Testament, God announced the definition of the word "seed" as being in the singular because it was describing Christ (see Gal. 3:16). But frequently the question is asked, "Who are those who are called the seed of Satan?" There was the great prophecy that there would be enmity between the seed of Satan and the Lord Jesus Christ. Who else are they but these Pharisees who so hated Christ and who schemed and planned His death? They and their modern offspring who do the same work are the ones who are called the seed of Satan.

In the book of the Psalms, there is the great prophetic picture of the death of the Lord Jesus Christ, which begins with the words He uttered on the cross, "My God, my God, why hast thou forsaken me?" (Ps. 22:1), and continues to the description of the agony of the Savior in His death. There is a phrase in the midst of the well-known description that needs a little explaining. We read, "Many bulls have compassed me: strong bulls of Bashan have beset me round" (v. 12). One commentator writes as follows of this passage, "The mighty ones in the crowd are here marked by the tearful eye of their victim. The priests, elders, scribes, Pharisees, rulers and captains bellowed round the cross like wild cattle, fed in the fat and solitary pastures of Bashan, full of strength and fury; they stamped and foamed around the innocent One, and longed to gore Him to death with their cruelties…" Yes, and adding one further word: that which most infuriates a bull is the sight and smell of blood. That which most infuriates the followers of the Pharisees in our day is the doctrine of salvation by the blood of Jesus Christ.

You may judge them by their fruits in respect to that doctrine. Go to the smooth-tongued preachers of modernism who occupy prominent pulpits throughout the land. Put to them this straight, unavoidable question, "Do you believe that men are eternally condemned to an eternity far from God unless they believe God's Word concerning the fact that He is forever satisfied with the work which the Lord Jesus Christ did upon the cross in shedding His blood?" You will see these modern bulls of Bashan chafe as under the goad.

These are more than mere children of wrath and children of disobedience. Those names belong to all men apart from Christ. But to these haters of the person of the Son of God, we read that our Lord says, "Ye are of your father, the devil, and the lusts of your father ye will do" (John 8:44). There is an awful warning here against these apostates. They are to be judged by their words. The idle words of which our Lord speaks, and of which men must give an accounting, are not, of course, to be interpreted as having any reference to the joys of a good sense of humor or the idle dreamings of rest hours and vacation days when the mind is lying fallow that it may produce yet stronger crops. These idle words are words of doctrine. These Pharisees had refused to give Christ His place as the eternal Jehovah manifest to destroy the works of the devil. This was to be the ground of their terrible condemnation. While these words may come to the attention of a few apostates, it is more than likely that the majority of unbelievers who read this belong to that good, substantial class of children of disobedience who have neglected, simply neglected, through love of sin or casual indifference, to accept the Lord Jesus Christ as their sin-bearer and only hope of salvation.

The message of the cross is the same today as when it first divided men into two groups. Take your stand very definitely with those who can look to God with full confidence and joy in Christ, that He has taken our sins upon Him that we might stand complete in that righteousness which He bestows, by faith, upon all who put their trust in His blood.

12
WHEN MEN THOUGHT CHRIST CRAZY

The men of Christ's day heard Him speak and saw Him work and were at a loss to account for Him. They were not willing to call Him God, for that would have meant the acceptance of His standards of righteousness and the consequent condemnation of themselves. They knew He was not an ordinary man. They asked Him whether He were Elijah, John or another of the prophets. They called Him a winebibber, as though to associate His sayings with those of some of His companions.

It must be realized that there was something in the life of the Lord Jesus Christ that was not intelligible on the basis of any ordinary human explanation. His enemies saw this and said that He had a demon. His friends and family tried to protect Him from this outrageous accusation by the equally foolish apology that He was a lunatic! What an example of dullness of perception of the human mind untouched by the Spirit of God! It is no wonder that God says, "But the natural man receiveth not the things of the Spirit of God: for they are foolishness unto him: neither can he know them, because they are spiritually discerned" (1 Cor. 2:14).

Can it be possible that His family and friends ever thought Him insane? The evidence that they did is clearly set forth in the Gospels, and we wish to tell the story and show what Jesus Christ said and did when men thought that He had gone crazy. The extreme significance of the scene will be realized when it is understood that these events occurred on that day when Jesus turned from His own, the Jews, in order to begin the series of events that was to take the Gospel to the whole world. The Pharisees had accused Him of being possessed of a demon. They said that He cast out demons by the aid of the prince of the demons. It was then that Jesus turned upon these pious hypocrites with such a blaze of wrath as this world had never seen until that moment, and which is but a faint foreshadowing of the day of the wrath of God when men shall cry to the rocks and the mountains to fall upon them that they might be hidden from the wrath of the Lamb.

Men thought that Jesus Christ was demon-possessed or crazy because He was God, moving, speaking, and working according to the methods that are beyond human understanding. God tells us through Isaiah, "For my thoughts are not your thoughts, neither are your ways my ways, saith the LORD. For as the heavens are higher than the earth, so are my ways higher than your ways, and my thoughts than your thoughts" (Isa. 55:8-9). Because there is this warfare of the divine against the human which is now in a fallen state, that which God does will always appear foolish to those who are untouched by the Spirit of God in regeneration. This is the reason for Christ's great imperative, "Ye must be born again" (John 3:7).

When the judgment phrases flashed forth from the lips of the Son of God, we can well imagine the scene among those who stood before Him. The Pharisees, who had just come from a council to determine methods to destroy Him, held back their fury with great difficulty and a little group of them moved toward Him with a question. As they came, it seems evident that someone from among the friends of His family must have moved off to send a messenger to His family, for we find His mother and His brethren on the scene shortly after this. But in the interval came the lying, face-saving question of the delegation from Jerusalem. "Master," they said, and we can almost hear the oily accents, "Master, we would see a sign from thee" (Matt. 12:38).

They did not want another sign. They had seen at least two that very morning. They had seen the man with the withered hand stretch it forth whole again. They had seen the man, blind and dumb, receive his sight and his voice. It was these miracles that had stirred the envy of their hearts to rage. It was this display of divine power that had caused them to say that He was working by the power of the devil.

The Lord Jesus knew their hearts and all their motives. This is why He answered them in these words which must have intensified their hatred and which must have confirmed some of His friends in the idea that perhaps He was out of His mind. For He turned upon these spokesmen of the Pharisees, saying, "An evil and adulterous generation seeketh after a sign; and there shall no sign be given to it, but the sign of the prophet Jonas: For as Jonas was three days and three nights in the whale's belly; so shall the Son of man be three days and three nights in the heart of the earth" (Matt. 12:39-40). Here again was the announcement of His death and His resurrection. They should have no other sign but that.

And certainly that was enough. Mohammed is dead and his tomb is known. Buddha and Confucius are dead and they shall not live again until the last judgment, but the Lord Jesus Christ is not dead. Three days was all that His body could be held by death, and that length of time only because it had pleased Him to set that time upon it, announcing it plainly in advance on more than one occasion.

Let us never forget that every week we celebrate the day of resurrection. Every week, we celebrate the fact that the living Lord Jesus Christ is the stone upon which our whole faith is built, as it is also the stumbling stone of all unbelief. This is the sign that is given to men who have doubts in their minds. This will measure the inner life of any man. It is a plough that goes deep into the hearts of men. Every time a man expresses an opinion about Jesus Christ, he is revealing what he is within himself. No other sign is given to men. No other miracle is necessary. If a man will not believe the evidence concerning the resurrection of the Lord Jesus Christ, there is nothing that can ever move his evil heart of unbelief. When the rich man in torment asked that a messenger be sent to his unbelieving brothers, he heard the terrible and solemn verdict upon their heart condition, "If they hear not Moses and the prophets, neither will they be persuaded, though one rose from the dead" (Luke 16:31). When the Word of God is rejected, the power of God is also rejected. These Pharisees had rejected the words of the Lord Jesus Christ. It is not astonishing that they attributed His power to the working of Satan.

As the Lord Jesus Christ spoke of His resurrection under the symbol of the great experience of Jonah, He went on to make a comparison. The generation that had heard Jonah had repented. The generation that heard Christ did not, yet He said, "...behold, a greater than Jonas is here." Then He gave them one more comparison. The Queen of Sheba had come a great distance to hear the wisdom of Solomon. But said Christ, "...behold, a greater than Solomon is here" (Matt. 12:41-42). There can be no mistaking the high and exalted position that Jesus Christ gave to Himself. Once more the foolishness of the objectors is manifested. There are those who pretend that Jesus did not claim to be more than man. But in a breath He chose the greatest preacher and the wisest king of the whole of Jewish history and calmly said that He Himself was their superior. This is indeed God Almighty or a lunatic.

Thus He stood and talked to the people. We can imagine what a stir this scene had caused among the humble folk of the town. They had suffered at the hands of the Pharisees but they had never dared to speak against them. The Lord said on another occasion that the Pharisees made long prayers for a pretence and devoured widows' houses (see Luke 20:47). Do you think that the hypocrisy of these pious scoundrels was not common gossip in the miserable homes of the poor whom they had defrauded? And now they heard Him speak this way of those whom they had learned to know as the most respected and the most infamous of Israel's leaders.

While He was talking thus to the people, His mother and His brethren arrived, evidently being hastily summoned by some friends. The picture, so far as the time sequence is concerned, is clearer in the Gospel according to Mark: "...his friends ... went out to lay hold on him: for they said, He is beside himself" (Mark 3:21). And after a short interval, "There came then his brethren and his mother, and, standing without, sent unto him, calling him..." (Mark 3:31).

There is no more pitiful scene in all the Bible than this one where Mary, the mother of Jesus, and her later sons came to the scene where the Lord Jesus was at work and tried to draw Him away from His task, even going so far as to think that He was crazy. It is remarkable how the Holy Spirit has kept us from the possibility of error, not only in considering events of the time of Christ but also in thinking in advance of the errors that have been added since His day. Mary, highly favored among women, and indeed the mother of the Lord Jesus Christ through the conception by the Holy Spirit, is not at all responsible for the terrible blasphemies that have been perpetrated in her name. A corrupt Church in the Middle Ages reversed the teachings of Christ Himself and put the mother in place of the Son, exalting an earthly relationship above that of a spiritual, and in her name, falsely, taught a poor and ignorant multitude to trust in her and look to her as a mediator. But here we find her outside while Christ is at grips with the Pharisees, coming with the rest of her sons which the Bible plainly says she bore to Joseph, and failing to understand this child. This is all the more astonishing, given that she should have known what Jesus was doing, because of His supernatural birth.

There are many words in the languages of earth to express the idea of insanity. It is interesting to note that such an authority as Roget gives only twenty-five words and phrases to describe sanity, but that he lists more than one hundred to describe insanity. While some of these are very picturesque in their description of the poor unfortunates who have lost their minds, there is none more interesting than this phrase used in the Bible to voice the thought of the friends and family of the Lord Jesus. They said, "He is beside himself" (Mark 3:21). There was a doubleness of personality in this man that opened Him to the charge of demon possession on the one side and lunacy on the other. Poor humanity! How far we all are from God by reason of our sin, and how we need the illumination of the Holy Spirit that we may understand spiritual matters.

Then the messenger of Mary and her sons came in. There must have been something in the attitude of the Pharisees—tight-lipped and furious—that frightened this messenger; something in the attitude of the crowd which feared the Pharisees but feared still more this Son of God Who had flashed His judgment-fire in their presence. We cannot read this passage in Matthew without seeing that the messenger approached Christ as one would approach a crazy man. If He can be persuaded to come away quietly, it may be possible to avoid a disagreeable scene. Has the moment of folly passed? Is He now in a lucid interval? Be careful! Such men are sometimes dangerous!

All this can be read between the lines without in any way adding to the message of the Word of God. Read their suggestion to Him in the light of such an attitude. Tremblingly, hesitatingly, they speak. "Behold … Thy … Thy mother and Thy … Thy brethren are without … desiring to speak with Thee…" (Matt. 12:47). We can almost hear the nervous, unconscious laugh which may have accompanied the plea.

Then He spoke. Did they jump back with fright? Certainly the words that fell from His lips might give every justification to a charge of insanity. For what could be a clearer indication of raving fantasy—or of divine purpose—than the words which Jesus now spoke. "Who is my mother? and who are my brethren?" (Matt. 12:48). In the hour when the wounded soldier on the battlefield becomes delirious with pain, his words run in the familiar channel of childhood and he calls for his mother. But this man, Jesus Christ, cries out, "Who is my mother?" What manner of Man is this? Is He, indeed, possessed or beside Himself?

No. This is divine purpose. And if ever we can see the indications of revelation from God it is surely here, for we have the clear revealing of the purpose of the coming of the Lord Jesus Christ to earth. Why did He leave Heaven's glory for earth's misery? "For the Son of man is come to seek and to save that which was lost" (Luke 19:10). "For even the Son of man came not to be ministered unto, but to minister, and to give his life a ransom for many" (Mark 10:45).

And all this is to be seen in the answer that He gave to Mary's messenger. "Who is my mother?" It is as though He said: "Forget these earthly relationships. In the moment of My death I will commit you to the care of John, that your old age may know no want, but now there are spiritual lessons to be taught." We must not forget that the only time in the Bible that Mary ever asked anything of the Lord Jesus, she was met with a rebuke. Now, for the great spiritual purposes involved in the change of dispensations, the Lord disowned the human relationship. "And he stretched forth his hand toward his disciples, and said, Behold my mother and my brethren!" (Matt. 12:49).

Earthly ties had been close in that Nazareth home. We have every right to believe that the Lord Jesus was a good son and a kind older brother to the family that came to Mary and Joseph. But when His ministry began He was misunderstood. We read the great prophetic passage where the Messiah speaks, "I am become a stranger unto my brethren, and an alien unto my mother's children. For the zeal of thine house hath eaten me up" (Ps. 69:8-9). John tells us that His brethren did not believe in Him at a certain moment of His ministry (see John 7:5). Later on they did believe. The book of the Acts tells us this fact. Mary had said when the angel first came to her with the news of the coming Child, "My soul doth magnify the Lord, And my spirit hath rejoiced in God my Saviour" (Luke 1:46-47). The brothers later believed in Him as their Savior.

There is a great lesson here: the Pharisees committed an unpardonable sin in thinking that He was possessed of a demon. But these loved ones, who considered Him insane, are all to be found numbered among the sinners saved by grace in the midst of the early Church. Truly, the grace of God is great.

But on that morning, when the crowd ringed Him about and some were saying He had a demon and others that He was crazy, He stretched forth His hand toward His disciples and said, "Behold my mother and my brethren." Spiritual relationships were to take the place of these human relationships. Then came another new word in the vocabulary of Jesus, a word that had never before been recorded on His lips in this sense. For when He had said, "Behold my mother and my brethren," He explained it by adding, "For whosoever shall do the will of my Father which is in heaven, the same is my brother, and sister, and mother" (Matt. 12:50). This is the fifth new word.

There is no word in the spiritual vocabulary that holds a sweeter place in the experience of the believer than this word "whosoever." Another time our Lord used it in a passage that must be known to millions and millions. It is the only verse in the Bible that many people know, and yet it is sufficient to take a man out of death and into life. For our Lord said to the Jewish leader who came to Him by night, "For God so loved the world, that he gave his only begotten Son, that whosoever believeth in him should not perish, but have everlasting life" (John 3:16).

Now, all of the Gospel message of John 3:16 is to be found in anticipation here in this passage spoken on the great day of rejection. It is true that back in the tenth chapter of Matthew we have the announcement, "Whosoever therefore shall confess me before men, him will I also confess before my Father which is in heaven" (Matt. 10:32), but the best students of the life of Christ place the occasion on which that announcement was made after the great day which we are studying.

Once more we must point out that the Gospel of the Lord Jesus Christ both condemns and invites. When Jesus Christ pronounced judgment upon the cities that had refused His ministry, He also gave the invitation, "Come unto me, all ye that labour and are heavy laden, and I will give you rest" (Matt. 11:28). Here again, we have this same division. He had just called the individual leaders of the Pharisees a "generation of vipers." The judgment is again balanced with this great invitation, "For whosoever shall do the will of my Father which is in heaven, the same is my brother, and sister, and mother."

This "whosoever," purely and simply, means you. No matter what your circumstances or status: God, the Lord and Savior Jesus Christ, invites you to full and free salvation. If you will do the will of the Father, you shall be as His mother and brethren to Him. And, in order that no one should be confused as to what the will of the Father might be, He has explained it most clearly. Men came to Him asking, "What shall we do, that we might work the works of God? Jesus answered and said unto them, This is the work of God, that ye believe on him whom he hath sent" (John 6:28-29). And again, "And this is the will of him that sent me, that everyone which seeth the Son, and believeth on him, may have everlasting life" (John 6:40).

There is a hymn that is sometimes sung in evangelistic services, the words of which include the phrase, "Whosoever surely meaneth me."[1] Can you say that for yourself? Do not stand with the crowd that put Christ among the devil's followers, as did the Pharisees. Do not stand with those who mistakenly supposed that He was beside Himself. Stand out with those whom He is willing to acknowledge as mother and brethren—His disciples who have believed that, in truth, this is the Son of God, come to die on the cross that we might go free.

---

[1]"Whosoever Meaneth Me." Words and music by J. Edwin McConnell, 1910.

13
THE DAY OF PARABLES

When the Lord Jesus Christ first began to speak in parables, His disciples wondered why He should thus change the method of His teaching. They asked Him, pointblank, why He was introducing this new method. He answered that it was because it was given to His disciples to understand the things He was about to teach, but that it was not given to the others—Phariees and the mixed multitude—who stood near at hand (see Matt. 13:11).

The proper understanding of the parables of the thirteenth chapter of Matthew will give to any Christian an insight into the real purpose of God during the age in which we live. A failure to understand these truths will cloud all other attempts to discern the meaning of Christ's teaching here.

This thirteenth chapter of Matthew begins with three words that give the key to the background of the parables: "The same day…" These parables were spoken on the great day of His rejection by the Pharisees. This fact is of such vital importance that we must ever keep it in mind. Since the precious sunset when this notable sabbath began, our Lord had pronounced His first judgment upon the cities where His mighty works had been done. It was at this time that He gave His first Gospel invitation. It was on the very same day on which the Pharisees had held their counsel against Him. It was on the very same day which

He had announced that He would now show mercy to the Gentiles. It was the day on which He first stripped the mask from the hypocritical leaders. It was the day on which He first used the wonderful word "whosoever" in a great Gospel call.

It would appear that most of these events had taken place in the morning. When it began to draw closer to noon, we may be sure that everyone wanted to go into the house to get away from the hot Palestinian sun. It is not hard to imagine the subject of conversation in a hundred homes that day. As the people sat down to their frugal meal, prepared the day before, you may be sure that many of them were talking about the events of the morning.

Jesus of Nazareth had called the Pharisees a "generation of vipers." On another occasion He told them that they were hypocrites, making long prayers for a pretence and devouring widows' houses. Do you not think that some of these widows had something to say that day as village gossip carried the tale into every house? Many people recognized that Jesus Christ had told the truth about these men and that He had had more than natural courage to tell that truth. And the miracles He had done must have created a profound impression. The man with the withered hand and the demon-possessed man who had regained sight and speech must have been the center of interested groups. So the house into which Jesus Christ went was watched.

The thirteenth chapter of Matthew is drawn against this background. "The same day went Jesus out of the house, and sat by the sea side." When He came out of the house there must have been many a small boy who darted down an alley or up a street to tell the news. The houses poured out their occupants who with common aim went down to the side of the Sea of Galilee where Jesus was sitting. How easily understood, therefore, is the second verse of the chapter, which reads,

"And great multitudes were gathered together unto him, so that he went into a ship, and sat; and the whole multitude stood on the shore."

So with a boat for a pulpit and the lakeside for the congregation, the Lord Jesus preached the second of His great discourses. But this is by far the most important of the sermons that He delivered, for it is this one that gives us the key to the understanding of the others. It is safe to say that the man who does not understand the sermon spoken from the boat will never understand the earlier sermon spoken on the mount, or the later one from the Mount of Olives.

"And he spake many things unto them in parables..." (v. 3). This is the sixth new word. And it was the first time He had ever spoken in parables. We may learn many great lessons from the parables themselves, but there are two great lessons to be found in the fact that He used this method. When His disciples asked Him why He spoke in parables He answered, "Because it is given unto you to know the mysteries of the kingdom of heaven, but to them it is not given. For whosoever hath, to him shall be given, and he shall have more abundance: but whosoever hath not, from him shall be taken away even that he hath. Therefore speak I to them in parables: because they seeing see not; and hearing they hear not, neither do they understand" (Matt. 13:11-13).

One writer labors with great effort to attempt to clear the Lord from what he would characterize "subtlety and cruelty." This writer says he would "most strenuously deny to be true" that interpretation which would intimate that the Lord Jesus "adopted the parabolic method with His hearers because He had abandoned them in anger, and that His purpose was to hide His truth so that they should not see it."[1]

In spite of all the explanation that is given by that great writer, we must nevertheless differ from him. For while we gladly admit that our

---

[1] Source unknown.

Lord did not abandon the Pharisees in anger, we must also admit that He had announced that they were abandoned in holiness and justice. These were the men who had said that He wrought His works because He was possessed of a demon. These were the men whose sin He had said would not be forgiven them in this world, nor in that to come. The reason that the Lord Jesus did speak in parables was in order to preserve His truth from those darkened minds, since they would not have believed though one rose from the dead. He would keep his pearls in the shell of parable so that they would not be trampled under foot. At the same time, there were simple folk among the multitude which gathered around Him, and these were capable of receiving the Word as He gave it forth. The Holy Spirit would be able to take the truth to their hearts and bring light out of darkness.

Christ's explanation was most categorical. It is given to some to know, and it is not given to others to know. But this is no arbitrary matter, He hastened to add. For the phrase which follows, and which has become so famous, is most simple when it is read in the light of all of Bible truth. "For whosoever hath, to him shall be given..." (v. 12). The world is familiar with that phrase which it has adopted as one of its own proverbs. But on the lips of the Lord it had a definite meaning. In the light of all the teaching of the New Testament, we may paraphrase it as follows: "For whosoever hath—new life in Christ through being born again—to him shall be given understanding of spiritual truths which the natural man cannot receive because they are foolishness unto him. Thus, this born-again man shall possess spiritual truth in abundance. But whosoever hath not—this new life which comes from God through faith in the Lord Jesus—from him shall be taken away even that which he hath—human intelligence which might make him exceedingly proficient in the study of the pagan philosophers and other writers."

Is this not the foregleam of the great statement of the epistles that "after that in the wisdom of God the world by wisdom knew not God, it pleased God by the foolishness of preaching to save them that believe" (1 Cor. 1:21)? If any man is to understand the parables or any other Christian truth, he must be born again.

It was on another occasion that a man of the Pharisees came to Jesus by night with an honest question about His work. Nicodemus thought that Jesus was a mere teacher come from God. This was the natural verdict of the heart that was untouched by the Spirit of God. The Lord swept away all such thought with His great answer, "Verily, verily, I say unto thee, Except a man be born again, he cannot see the kingdom of God" (John 3:3). Christ was not a teacher come from God. He was God come to teach. It was necessary for Nicodemus, as it is necessary for each one of us today, to recognize, "That which is born of the flesh is flesh; and that which is born of the Spirit is spirit " (John 3:6). So it is only by the supernatural mind that men can understand supernatural thoughts.

Certainly, the truths that Jesus Christ was about to announce in the parables are truths that need the light of the Holy Spirit. He must shine on hearts that are yielded to God before they can be understood. For it is undoubtedly true that there are many, many Christians, born again, who garble the meaning of these parables and who, therefore, go wrong in their understanding of much of the deeper truth of Scripture. This comes, of course, from the fact that saved men frequently study the Bible solely with the human spirit instead of the guidance of the Holy Spirit.

Christ said that these parables were given so that His own might have at their disposal the understanding of "the mysteries of the kingdom of heaven." What does this mean? There are many people who read the Bible superficially. Some of the finest distinctions of Scripture truth are lost upon them. They have not studied to show themselves approved unto God, workmen that need not to be ashamed, rightly dividing the

Word of truth (see 2 Tim. 2:15). To them there is evidently no reason for studying the Bible closely to see if there is any real difference between the Kingdom of Heaven and the Kingdom of God, or if there is any difference between the Kingdom of Heaven and what Christ calls here, "the mysteries of the kingdom of heaven."

Christ Himself gave great importance to the shades of meaning. He based His doctrine of life after death on the difference between the present and the past tense of a verb in the book of the Psalms (see Matt. 22:32). Time and again, He based the whole of His teaching on a spiritual rather than upon a material meaning of symbols. We see this, for instance, when He spoke of the resurrection of His body. Even His followers thought that He spoke of the literal temple built by Herod (see John 2:21).

So here, there is a great difference between the Kingdom of Heaven and the mysteries of the Kingdom of Heaven. Let us define our terms. The Kingdom of God is the rule of God over the universe in its entirety. It includes the omnipotence of God, so that even Satan and all that he does is bound up within that great, all-reaching term. It stretches from eternity to eternity. Once or twice, however, the phrase is used, as in Christ's conversation with Nicodemus, in a much narrower sense, of spiritual insight into spiritual matters.

The Kingdom of Heaven, on the other hand, is a material, literal Kingdom upon the earth. It is the rule of the heavens over the earth. It is found described throughout the whole of the Old Testament. Messiah is to be its King, Jerusalem its capital. The last book in the Bible limits its duration to one thousand years. It is the millennial Kingdom. It is primarily Jewish, though it shall include, of course, all the inhabitants of the earth. But the promises of the Kingdom were earthly and Jewish.

This is the Kingdom that John the Baptist came preaching. This is the Kingdom that Jesus Himself was offering unto the Jews. He came unto

His own with the offer, but they rejected the righteous principles upon which it was to be founded and so He postponed its establishment. On this great day of crisis that we are studying, He had practically announced the withdrawal of that earlier offer. That Kingdom will be postponed for many hundreds of years. It is that which Christ will establish at His second coming.

But what is going to happen in the meantime? Here we come to "the mysteries of the kingdom of heaven." For between the rejection of Christ by His own people and His return there is a great lapse of time that already has run nineteen centuries. Every time we sit at the communion table, we look backward to the Lord's death and forward "till he come." It is this great period that constitutes the Kingdom in mystery.

Do not be confused by the modern meaning of the word "mystery." In the Bible sense of the term there is nothing mysterious whatsoever in what are called the mysteries of Scripture. Eleven different times the word is used to describe some truth which is being explained. The world interprets mystery as something that is hidden and covered. Darkness shrouds the true solution. But a mystery in the Bible is a truth that has been hidden but which is now revealed. The eleven subjects that are thus described are subjects that may be fully studied and readily understood, because God Himself has been pleased to reveal the secret. When a secret has been told there is no more riddle to be guessed.

This is what Christ is doing here. He is announcing in advance what is to occur between the time of His first coming and the time of His second coming. For while the actual earthly Kingdom has been postponed for more than nineteen hundred years, there have been people in every generation and in every nation who have given themselves to the salvation which was presented by the death of Jesus Christ. These form the very heart of the Kingdom in mystery. The truth is penetrating from heart to heart. But this body of true believers finds itself in the midst of a great ecclesiastical organization that men call "the Church." And this organization, in turn, is in the midst of a chaotic mass that we might call Christendom, which is a fragment of the whole world system. All this is in view in this thirteenth chapter of Matthew.

But someone may wonder if we have the right to be so positive when we state that these parables have nothing whatsoever to do with the Kingdom that has been described in the Old Testament and which must yet come upon the earth if God is to remain true. Later on in this chapter of parables, there is a verse of paramount importance in the understanding of Scriptural truth and in the establishing of the fact that we are living in a parenthesis between two literal comings of Christ.

When the Lord had announced the parables of the sower, the wheat and the tares, the mustard seed, and the leaven, He paused before going back into the house and the Holy Spirit, through Matthew, spoke a verse so plain that it fixes a definite time limit upon the sphere of the parables. Henceforth, it is impossible to confuse them with anything that has ever been written before. For the Holy Spirit says, "All these things spake Jesus unto the multitude in parables; and without a parable spake he not unto them: That it might be fulfilled which was spoken by the prophet, saying, I will open my mouth in parables; I will utter things which have been kept secret from the foundation of the world" (Matt. 13:34-35). There is one phrase that we must insist upon again so that its tremendous teaching may not be lost. Christ our Lord said, "I will open my mouth in parables; I will utter things which have been kept secret from the foundation of the world."

Everyone who wishes to understand the Bible must catch the import of that declaration. It is the plain announcement that there is no connection between the parables taught by the Lord Jesus Christ and the teachings of the Old Testament. It is important that that truth be digested fully. Draw out of it all the logical conclusions. These parables individually are spoken concerning "the kingdom of heaven," which is defined here as "the mysteries of the kingdom of heaven." Our Lord says that these parables are presenting new truth. Therefore, they have nothing to do with any phase of truth that is to be found in the Old Testament. The Kingdom in view here is not the Kingdom that had been prophesied, but an aspect of God's dealings that had been hidden from man until now God was ready to reveal His purpose to men.

The Kingdom that is described in the Old Testament is a visible, earthly Kingdom. Christ sits upon the throne of His father, David (see Isa. 9:7); He reigns upon the holy hill of Zion (see Ps. 2:6); in a glorious and visible manner (see Isa. 24:23); and His rule is over the earth in the same manner that any empire holds sway (see Ps. 72:8; Zech. 14:9). Natural conditions are to be entirely changed. Desert places will become gardens and beautiful trees shall replace thorns and thistles (see Isa. 35:1; 55:13). The animal world is to undergo complete reorganization at the hands of the Creator. Poison shall disappear from the serpent and the carnivorous animals shall lose their murderous instincts (see Isa. 11:6-9).

All of these promises must be fulfilled. If they are not, we can have no confidence in the Bible. If this change in the earth, in its creatures and in man himself does not take place, then we might as well throw our Bibles away, for we could have no confidence at all in the promises concerning life after death or in the keeping power of our risen Lord. In fact, the whole of the structure of confidence in God must be destroyed if He is proved untrue in any particular. Any attempt to explain these promises in a fashion that destroys their literalness is to trifle with the Bible, and to destroy its trustworthiness.

But all confusion is cleared away if we see that the Lord Jesus came presenting this Kingdom, but that when He was refused, the offer was withdrawn. We must see that now our Lord is in the position of that nobleman in one of His parables, who went into a far country to receive a kingdom and to return (see Luke 19:12). In the meantime, we are in the parenthesis described in these parables of the thirteenth chapter of Matthew.

To put it in the simplest language, we may state it thus: These parables, spoken on the day of His great crisis, are a summary of the history of the Church age. Here we find Church history written in advance. And the only way to study the parables of the thirteenth chapter of Matthew is to read them as a declaration by Christ of the course of the age in which we are living and then to check up by referring to the great outlines of Church history to find whether or not His prophecies are in accord with what we know to be the historical facts.

There is not space to discuss the parables in detail here. That would require a volume in itself. Suffice it to say, here, that the picture of this age is so clearly drawn in these parables that there can be no excuse for the Christian who is found to be working counter to the revealed plan of God.

In a word it may be said that we are told that this age is to be one of missionary enterprise and evangelistic effort. The Christian is to witness, scattering the Word everywhere. But he must do so with the certain knowledge that his preaching will be rejected by the vast majority of men. There is not one line in the Bible that can be made to teach that the world will be converted by the preaching of the Gospel. There is not one line in all the Bible that would justify the slogan, "The World for Christ." There is not one line in the Bible that would support the claim of those who think it their province to try to make the unbelieving world good by legislation or decree or social effort. There is also no place for the claim of those who would seek to establish a state religion of any kind upon any nation.

Rather, we find that the Gospel is to be preached to individuals; that our slogan must be "Christ for the world." The cross of Jesus Christ provides redemption and we are to take that message out as ambassadors for Christ in the midst of a world of darkness. We are to shine as lights in the world, holding forth the Word of life (see Phil. 2:16). Ours is the message of the cross and the blood, and of salvation for individuals. While the day of grace is still running its course, this salvation is for you.

14
THE LAST NEW WORD

It can readily be seen that the day of official rejection by the leaders of Israel was a great one in the life of our Lord Jesus. It called into His vocabulary an entirely new set of words. "He came unto his own, and his own received him not. But ..." But... "woe upon [the cities]." But ..."come unto me." But ... "Gentiles." But ... "generation of vipers." But ... "whosoever." But ... "parables."

The break was complete. He would go on preaching and teaching, healing the sick and raising the dead, but His face was now set for Jerusalem. From all eternity He had known that He would come to die. The honest presentation of the Kingdom was to work out in His rejection and He could say in truth, "...the Son of man came...to give his life a ransom for many" (Mark 10:45). The dispensation of law would not come to its final end until He cried, "It is finished" (John 19:30), but already the hammer had clicked into place, ready to strike the hour.

One more new word came into His vocabulary. It was not spoken on the great day of rejection, but some time later. How much later we may not be able to determine, but that is not important. The longer one lives with the Bible, the more certain he becomes that God has ordered His material in the way in which we find it in order to present the full-rounded portrait that we find in each portion of the Word. As it is, naturally, Matthew who has told us the details of Messiah's rejection tells us the last new word here.

He fed the five thousand, departed for a season into Gentile country where He healed the daughter of the Gentile woman, and returned to Galilee where He fed the four thousand. Then a great symbolic act occurred with words that are most important. He took His disciples, alone, out into Gentile country again. This is a demonstration that His own had failed to receive Him, but that He would have true confession and worship, nevertheless.

Christ asked His disciples, "Whom do men say that I the Son of man am?" (Matt. 16:13). He knew, of course, the thoughts and words of all men, but He was about to draw from them a most vital confession. He was not referring to the statements of the Pharisees who had said that He worked through the power of Satan. The question revealed, first of all, the state of the common gossip of the multitudes who had eaten His created bread and who had seen His miracle power. Truly they were blinded. The best that they could see in the Lord was expressed in the thought that He must be the reincarnation of some one of the mighty men of old whose names they knew from their childhood teaching of the Scriptures. Some said John the Baptist, who had recently been beheaded; some said Elijah, some said Jeremiah, though there was no similarity between the two; and then the guesses scattered off among the other prophets. This is just another example of the stupidity of the religious. These people had not spiritual discernment, that rarest of all of the gifts of the Spirit.

The disciples who were talking with Jesus were not responsible for the false opinions of the people. If we are reporting opinion, it will be necessary to recount the whole octave of unbelief. And we must not forget that unbelief may be complimentary to Christ without being true to Him. Adjectives mean absolutely nothing until they are measured by the noun which they modify. You may hear it said that a certain woman is the most charming, beautiful, cultured and noblest—and those adjectives are indeed superlatives that anyone would be proud to own and deserve; but no woman would desire to be called the most charming, beautiful, cultured and noblest prostitute. The adding of the reprehensible noun changes the value of the adjectives. So men may give to Christ the finest adjective in the vocabulary of praise, but unless they have the right noun to go with their adjectives, all that they have said may be sheer ignorance, or else blasphemy, and certainly rejection.

Ministers who are members in good standing of great evangelical denominations have been known to sit tranquilly on the platform of fellowship meetings where representatives of various faiths have passed compliments about the Lord Jesus Christ. In a meeting of a fellowship of faiths an Oriental rose to say, "Jesus was once an object of such hatred that I would spit when I heard His Name, but now I am willing to place Him on a level with Buddha and Confucius."

The world knows how to measure such statements, and has created a proverb to cover them. This type of "compliment" damns with faint praise. Let us not forget that the Lord Jesus Christ will have none of it. He will have the full rank and title that goes with His position and being, or He will accept nothing. This is the heart meaning of the incident where He was approached with the address, "Good Master." The Lord Jesus was not willing to be called "good" by one who would not believe in Him as God. So He refused the adjective. "Why callest thou me good? there is none good but one, that is, God" (Matt. 19:16-17). It was not that Jesus was denying His own intrinsic goodness. It was that He would not be a party to such slippery thinking. If the ruler wished to call Christ good, then let him call Him God; but if he refused to call Him God, then let him learn that the compliment is not acceptable. There is no alternative.

The disciples, by their answer to Jesus' first question, demonstrated that they were good reporters. They were able to echo public opinion. But Jesus asked a much more important question. "But whom say ye that I am?" (Matt. 16:15). This is the question for which the incident was opened.

"But whom say ye that I am?" Peter answered and said, "Thou art the Christ, the Son of the living God" (v. 16). This was indeed a breath–taking reply. This was saying that Jesus of Nazareth is the Anointed One, the promise of the Old Testament Scriptures. It was the equivalent of saying that He is the second person of the Godhead. How is this statement to be accepted? What will be the reaction of an honest man to a great claim on his behalf? I know men who are so humble and so true that if any exaggerated statement is made concerning their activities or their honors, they are quick to correct the fault and reduce their own glory and position to the strictest minimum.

Let those who claim that Jesus Christ was not God judge Him, then, by the ordinary standards of modest gentlemen. Peter cried out, "Thou art the Christ, the Son of the living God." Jesus Christ did not withdraw from the statement. There was no shrinking away from its implications. Rather there was a full-rounded acceptance of the position and all it involves as Christ said that Peter's answer was God's revealed truth.

It was Simon Peter who answered for the group. This point must be taken into consideration as we hear his reply. The reason that Simon Peter answered was because of his nature and character. I like Simon Peter very much. He is perhaps the most American of all the characters in the Bible. He is quick to talk, so quick that frequently he has nothing or worse than nothing to say. You will be surprised, perhaps, if you read the four Gospels and copy down every word recorded as spoken by Peter. Almost everything he ever said was a mistake. "Lo, we have left all and followed thee; what shall we have therefore?" "Be it far from thee, Lord: this shall never be to thee." "Lord, if it be thou, bid me come unto thee on the water." "Yes, my Master pays tribute." "The crowd press thee, and how sayest thou, who touched me?" "Lord, it is good for us to be here; let us make three tabernacles…" "How oft shall my brother sin against me, and I forgive him?" "Though all men deny thee, yet will not I." "Thou shalt never wash my feet. Lord, not my feet only but my hands and my head." "I know him not." The disciples had undoubtedly taken Peter's measure. They knew that he was a rude, uncouth, impertinent fellow but, withal, very human and lovable.

Back of his question, "How oft shall my brother sin against me, and I forgive him?" is possibly the echo of many a quarrel that a man of such hot-headed temperament must have drawn upon himself. So it was necessary that the Lord Jesus make a comment upon Peter's answer to the great question, lest the disciples discount the truth since it was spoken by Peter.

And the comment was to the effect that Peter's answer was not the product of human logic and reflection but that it was, definitely, a supernatural revelation. "Blessed art thou, Simon Bar-jona: for flesh and blood hath not revealed it unto thee, but my Father which is in heaven" (Matt. 16:17). Here we have an illustration of that truth which was to be expressed later through the writing of St. Paul, "…no man can say that Jesus is the Lord [i.e., Jehovah], but by the Holy Ghost" (1 Cor. 12:3). Peter was testifying to the deity of the Lord Jesus Christ. This fact governs all that follows, and settles forever one of the most argued questions of the centuries.

To say that Jesus is the Christ, the Son of the living God, is a great confession of faith. To call Him the Christ, which is merely the Greek word for the Hebrew "Messiah," is to say that He is the center and object of the whole of the Old Testament with its mighty prophecies. Peter was acknowledging more than the person of Christ; he was confessing his own personal faith in Him; and it is a personal faith in Him as the Son of the living God. In the Gospel of John, Jesus spoke of Himself as having life in Himself, even as the Father hath life in Himself (see John 5:26).

It is worthwhile noticing that this is the first personal confession of faith in Jesus Christ that we find in this Gospel. Peter, through a divine revelation from the Father, spoke forth his faith in the living Lord Jesus Christ. He did not understand just then all that he was saying. But, as a baby may be very much alive without knowing anything about the biological process of life, so Peter was alive in Christ, then, through faith which was not of himself, but which was the gift of God.

So the Lord Jesus Christ immediately announced the future Church. This is the last of these new words in the vocabulary of the Lord Jesus: "the Church." Not the organization but the organism; the living, vital body of all true believers in Jesus as the Christ, the Son of the living God.

This is the occasion of the first mention of the Church, and the true meaning of the Church and its foundations can be found in the incident itself. The full statement is as follows: "Blessed art thou, Simon Bar-jona: for flesh and blood hath not revealed it unto thee, but my Father which is in heaven. And I say also unto thee, That thou art Peter, and upon this rock I will build my church; and the gates of hell shall not prevail against it" (Matt. 16:17-18). There is only one Church and there is only one way to get into it. The one Church is composed of all those who put their whole trust in nothing less than the person and the work of the Lord Jesus Christ as their own personal Savior.

What a contrast between Peter's confession of faith and the rejection on the part of the leaders of Israel, those Pharisees who had been seeking to trap the Lord and who had finally come to the place of open rejection of His claims! Peter believed, and so he was called blessed by the Lord.

And the Lord is ready to say precisely the same thing to any man in our day who believes. Your name may be John, or William, or Elizabeth, or Catherine; but if you come to the place where you look in trust to the Lord Jesus Christ, accepting Him as your own sin bearer, you will know what it is to realize that God, through His Word, is saying to you, "And blessed art thou, John, or William, or Elizabeth, or Catherine, or whatever your name may be; for flesh and blood hath not revealed it to thee, but My Father Who is in Heaven."

Thus the believer finds himself blessed; blessed with all spiritual blessings in the heavenly places in Christ Jesus (see Eph. 1:3). It is when we have put our trust in Jesus Christ as our Lord that we are counted as being on the rock, Christ Jesus. We would not want to bring this study to a close without asking you if you have been born again, if you have put your trust in Christ, and in Him alone.

As we have seen that Peter was merely the first of a line of multitudes who know what it is to find their blessing in Christ, so we can go on with the phrase. For, as the Lord spoke to Peter using the future tense, "…upon this rock I will build my church," so He speaks to us using the past and present tenses. We acknowledge that Jesus Christ is our Lord and Savior. He blesses us and we may take the Bible and hear Him say to us through its pages, "You have acknowledged Me as Lord and Savior. You are John, or William, or Elizabeth, or Catherine. It is upon this rock that I have built and am building My Church; and the gates of Hell shall not prevail against it." It is upon this rock, His deity. For let us be very definite and sure about this matter once again. There is no foundation other than that of the Lord Jesus Christ Himself.

Perhaps the most amazing thing in Scriptural misinterpretation is that some people think that Christ built the Church on Peter. It is beyond our comprehension to understand how anybody who is capable of understanding plain English prose, let alone the Greek, could ever make out of this passage that Peter was the foundation. We shall see in a moment that Peter himself denies that he is the foundation and says that Christ is the only rock.

The original language is, of course, absolutely beyond question. Here is how it reads: "...thou art Petros [masculine gender–the little quarried stone], and upon this Petra [neuter gender, the great living rock of the mountain], I will build my church." Go to any institution of higher learning where you might find a Jew who knows the Greek tongue. He would not be biased in any way because his would be an outside position, neutral in questions of New Testament interpretation. He would tell you that the grammar of the passage demands a translation that will make it understood that the Church is built upon the truth of Christ's deity which Peter had acknowledged, and not at all on Peter the man.

Some time after this incident occurred, Christ died on the cross, was buried and rose again from the dead. He ascended into Heaven and sent the Holy Spirit to fill the lives of those who believed in Him as Savior and Lord. In Acts 4, Peter, along with John, were arrested and brought before the Sanhedrin, the highest court of the Jews, for healing the lame man in the Name of Jesus at the Beautiful Gate (see Acts 3:1-10). As Peter stood there before the leaders of his people, he cried out,

> Be it known unto you all, and to all the people of Israel, that by the name of Jesus Christ of Nazareth, whom ye crucified, whom God raised from the dead, even by him doth this man stand here before you whole. This is the stone which was set at nought of you builders, which is become the head of the corner. Neither is there salvation in any other: for there is none other name under heaven given among men, whereby we must be saved (Acts 4:10-12).

This is the stone: the risen Lord Jesus Christ. And some thirty years later, when Peter was writing his first epistle, he said, "If so be ye have tasted that the Lord is gracious. To whom coming, as unto a living stone ..." To *whom* coming (referring to Jesus); Peter would never have claimed to be the stone. So he concluded, "To whom coming, as unto a living stone, disallowed indeed of men, but chosen of God, and precious, Ye also, as living stones, are built up a spiritual house, an holy priesthood, to offer up spiritual sacrifices, acceptable to God by Jesus Christ. Wherefore also it is contained in the scripture, Behold, I lay in Sion a chief corner stone, elect, precious: and he that believeth on him shall not be confounded" (1 Pet. 2:3-6).

We once saw a picture of a cabin that had been built out of posts and logs which, after they were cut, took root and put forth branches, so that the cabin was literally a growing house. This is the wonderful illustration that Peter explains to us here, and which is the heart of the great passage in Matthew. Just as that wood grew so that the house was a growing house, so, because we are from Christ the living stone, we shall grow in Him as living stones.

The Church, then, is not to be considered as an organization, but as the organism, composed, not of members who have joined something, but of believers who have been made alive in Christ through the new birth. The Church is built upon the truth of Christ. The fact of His identity is sufficient foundation for the Church. Because He is the ever-living God He is able to save to the uttermost, them who come unto God by Him (see Heb. 7:25).

In all generations the spiritual body of believers has been quick to see this great truth and to build all its hope upon it. In all centuries, the Church has had its great hymns that may have changed from language to language, but which still sing the same thoughts to the changing harmony of the ages.

God's Word about the Lord Jesus Christ: this is the solid foundation of the Church of Jesus Christ. And this supernatural revelation God has confirmed by His oath, so that "by two immutable things, in which it was impossible for God to lie, we might have a strong consolation, who have fled for refuge to lay hold upon the hope set before us: Which hope we have as an anchor of the soul..." (Heb. 6:18-19).

There is one last great lesson that we must consider for a moment. We do not know whether or not Peter became puffed up with pride because the Lord Jesus so signally honored his great confession. We do know that Jesus began to talk about His own death which was to come to Him at the cross and that Peter rebuked Him for speaking of it. "From that time forth," we read, "began Jesus to shew unto his disciples, how that he must go unto Jerusalem, and suffer many things of the elders and chief priests and scribes, and be killed, and be raised again the third day. Then Peter took him, and began to rebuke him, saying, Be it far from thee, Lord: this shall not be unto thee. But he turned, and said unto Peter, Get thee behind me, Satan: thou art an offence unto me: for thou savourest not the things that be of God, but those that be of men" (Matt. 16:21-23).

We see three absolutely different types of utterance coming from the human lips of Simon Peter. We see him quick to speak out the emptiness of his own heart and mind in utter foolishness; we see him as the mouthpiece of divine revelation; and in the next breath we see him as the mouthpiece of Satan. Does not this teach us one of the most important lessons in the whole realm of spiritual matters? That lesson is that we cannot have confidence in the word of any man, not even in that of a "St. Peter."

There are three kinds of spirits. All three of them speak from the lips of Peter. The human spirit can give human thoughts. The Holy Spirit can give divine revelation. The spirit of Satan is the spirit of antichrist.

All three spoke through Peter. All human beings are subject to speaking the thought of Satan or the merely human thought. All believers in Christ are, in addition, capable of speaking the truth of God. But we can have no final confidence in any human being or in any organization, ecclesiastic or otherwise, that is composed of mere human beings.

God therefore has given us the Bible as the Supreme Court, from which there is no appeal. We certainly do not want anyone in the world to believe spiritual truth merely because it comes from us. But the ideal attitude for the reader is that of the Christians in Berea. These are called more noble than those elsewhere, "in that they received the word with all readiness of mind." But that is not all. For even though it was St. Paul speaking under the guidance of the Holy Spirit, they "searched the scriptures daily, whether those things were so" (Acts 17:11). We are personally convinced of the truth of all that we teach. But we desire in those whom we teach that attitude which looks behind any human personality and goes to the Word of God alone as the supreme and final authority for all truth.

Christ came unto His own people, the Jews, with the offer of fulfillment of all that the Scriptures promised concerning the Kingdom of God on earth. The leaders, because of their unregenerate hearts, rejected the righteousness, holiness and justice which must be at the base of all of God's gifts to man. His own people received Him not. But the central portion of Matthew's Gospel records the great turning point in the life of the Lord. A new vocabulary to fit a new mission with a new emphasis and a new message. "His own" henceforth takes on a double meaning. His own of the earth will always be the physical children of Abraham, but His heavenly people are also His own, whom He loved unto the end (see John 13:1).

Today, our Lord is in Heaven. The new body, the Church, is being called out of the world. We wait for our Lord from Heaven Who shall take us to Himself before returning to this earth to consummate every promise and plan which He has formed for His earthly people, and to establish His Kingdom, through power, over all the earth.

Donald Grey Barnhouse was, for half a century, one of the most widely acclaimed American preachers. Scholarly exposition and a popular approach marked his teaching. An unyielding faith, devotion to Christ, innovation, and great energy marked his ministry.

Although some found him overly abrupt and sometimes controversial, his zeal for the kingdom of God made him an exciting and captivating speaker. His elocutionary ability sprung from his careful speech, friendly manner, vivid analogies and most of all from his faithful exposition of the Scriptures. He was able to make the Bible relevant to the modern man. In fact his sermons have grown no less relevant to those who hear or read them today.

Dr. Barnhouse was one of the pioneers of radio preaching in the 1920s. Eventually he launched his own network program, The Bible Study Hour. In 1949 he began his famous study of Romans which continued each week for nearly twelve years until his death. This broadcast continues to air as *Dr. Barnhouse & the Bible*.

The written word was also part of Barnhouse's ministry. He wrote many articles and authored more than a dozen books. He was founder and editor-in-chief of *Eternity* magazine. He displayed remarkable insight in his evaluation of the meaning of events for church and nation.

For over thirty years Dr. Barnhouse conducted a weekly Bible study class in New York City. More than five hundred people attended. The demand for his services as a speaker and a conference leader was international.

His ministry was a varied one. For thirty-three years until his death he served as the pastor of Philadelphia's Tenth Presbyterian Church. There his influence was realized in many young lives that were directed into the ministry and the foreign mission field.

WHAT IS THE ALLIANCE?

The Alliance of Confessing Evangelicals is a coalition of believers who hold to the historic creeds and confessions of the Reformed faith and proclaim biblical doctrine in order to foster a Reformed awakening in today's Church.

Since its start in 1949, the Alliance has reached millions of people worldwide with resources that share the Gospel, proclaim biblical doctrine, engage with culture, and equip the Church. This work is carried out through broadcasting, events, and publishing.

Broadcasting began with **The Bible Study Hour** now featuring James Boice. Also airing throughout America and online at **Alliancenet. org** is **Every Last Word** featuring Philip Ryken, **Dr. Barnhouse & the Bible** with Donald Barnhouse, **InPerspective** and **Fresh Bread** with Harry Reeder, **Mortification of Spin** with Carl Trueman and Todd Pruitt, **Theology on the Go** with Jonathan Master and James Dolezal, **Kids Talk Church History**, and **Hear the Word of God** with Eric Alexander.

Publishing includes both print and digital media. Books from trustworthy authors, such as *The Word and the Way: Living the Christian Life* by Eric Alexander, and a wide variety of audio, affordable booklets, books, and eBooks by nationally known pastors and theologians are available at **ReformedResources.org**.

Place for Truth is our free "go-to" biblical/theological resource. **reformation21** provides cultural and church critique. Our online daily devotionals include **Think and Act Biblically** from Dr. Boice and **MatthewHenry.org,** fostering biblical prayer.

Events include the **Philadelphia Conference on Reformed Theology**, the oldest continuing national Reformed conference in North America, as well as regional events designed to encourage, embolden, and equip the Church.

For more, visit AllianceNet.org.